Composition Guide

Century College English Department

Contributors
Rich Kuss
Kathy Saylor
Kim Gaffney
Sue Taylor
Laurel Hagge

KENDALL/HUNT PUBLISHING COMPANY
4050 Westmark Drive   Dubuque, Iowa   52002

Contents

Acknowledgments

Thank you to writers and editors of the original *Century College English Handbook*.

We also thank the following individuals for their permission to use their essays*:

Todd Woolson for his narrative, "Erin's Wrath"

Tina Malsbender for the persuasive research paper, "School Uniforms for Public School Children"

Lori Stifter for the poetry analysis, "Do Not Fear Death."

Annemarie Solon for the documented essay, "More than Movies."

*Student essays have been edited for publication.

Chapter One: Composition Courses at Century College

The sequence of composition courses at Century College is designed to produce competent and careful writers. The four courses in the sequence are: English 0080, *Basic Writing and Grammar*; English 0090, *Introduction to Writing*; English 1021, *Composition I*; and English 1022, *Composition II*. Each course within the sequence builds upon the skills mastered in the previous one. Your assessment scores or your completed coursework will determine your placement in these courses.

The two courses covered in this book are the college-level (transfer eligible) courses, English 1021 and English 1022.

English 1021 has **both** a reading prerequisite **and** a writing prerequisite. **Each** of these prerequisites can be fulfilled **either by placement test scores or by coursework**. You must complete **both** prerequisites to enroll in any of these courses.

Course Descriptions

English 1021

Composition I is a four-credit, college-level course required of all students in degree programs. No matter your major, you will be writing papers, reports, exams, case studies, class notes, and lab reports in your courses. When you have finished college, you will be applying for jobs in technical, business, or other professional fields that require strong writing skills. Because competent writing is so important, colleges and universities require students to take composition courses. In fact, a course similar to English 1021 is required in virtually all degree programs at every accredited college in the nation.

If you are ready for English 1021, you have already learned many skills necessary for good expository writing. You know how to discover ideas for your writing, to organize and present your ideas in a clear and effective way, to keep your readers and your purpose in mind as you write, to improve your writing by rethinking and rewriting, to give helpful responses to others about their writing, to follow the conventions of standard English, and to evaluate your own writing.

Your English 1021 instructors will assume that you have mastered these skills. They will ask you to strengthen these skills through practice; to discover alternative ways of constructing sentences, paragraphs, and essays; to select the best writing strategy for your particular purpose; and to study style and structure in model essays. If you are successful in English 1021, you will be working much harder on your writing at the end of the course than you did at the beginning because you will have learned that all good writing is the result of hard work. You will have discovered that writing is not an inborn talent but a skill that improves with practice. You will have developed skills that will be useful in college and profitable on the job, and you will have experienced the satisfaction that comes from expressing yourself well in writing.

The format of English 1021 varies from one section to another. In most sections, you will meet three days a week in the classroom, **and** you will spend an average of **one hour a week in the Writing Center**. (This requirement is explained further in the following section). You may also have individual or small-group conferences with your instructor several times during the term. In evening, weekend, and some weekday sections of 1021, all four credit hours will be met through actual time spent in class or in conference with the instructor.

The foremost requirement in English 1021 is to complete all major writing assignments. Testing, texts, and teaching methods may vary from one section to another, but the writing requirement is the same. Consequently, failure to turn in all writing assignments may result in a failing grade for the course.

At least one writing assignment will focus on the writing of a **documented essay** that includes research materials to develop and support your own thesis. Chapter Three of this handbook deals with the methods and skills needed for this assignment.

Following are the skills expected of all students completing English 1021 at the "C" level. Every skill may not be demonstrated on every assignment, but you should be able to demonstrate **all** of these skills by the end of the course:

The student's writing process
- allows the student to adapt to different writing situations
- involves invention and the use of writing as a tool for learning and discovery
- involves experimentation
- involves genuine and substantial revision
- improves the student's writing through multiple drafts
- involves careful editing and proofreading of own work

The student's knowledge about writing and rhetoric includes
- an understanding of basic rhetorical concepts, such as purpose and audience
- an understanding of conventions of expository writing, especially the concept of thesis
- an understanding that written documents can be analyzed to see how they work
- an awareness that formal rules for acknowledging sources exist

The student's finished writing
- demonstrates an awareness of the connection between purpose and audience
- responds appropriately to the assignment
- presents a thesis and stays focused on that thesis
- supports the thesis with appropriate and sufficient details, examples, and explanation, including evidence beyond the writer's personal experience
- uses well-developed and unified paragraphs with carefully constructed sentences
- articulates complex thought appropriate to basic college-level work
- presents a logical and coherent argument
- has an appropriate structure, including an effective introduction and conclusion
- is organized and uses transitions effectively
- shows an awareness of style in its use of language
- is presented as finished so that it is easily read and follows any stated guidelines for format
- is grammatically and mechanically competent, especially regarding sentence boundaries and potentially distracting errors

English 1022

Composition II requires you to write essays that have many of the same characteristics as the essays you wrote in English 1021: a clear thesis, logical organization, well-developed paragraphs, and effective sentences.

In addition to being a composition course, English 1022 is an introduction to the study of literature. The literary content of the course will vary from one section of 1022 to another, but all instructors will ask you to write essays related to literature.

You will also write at least one documented paper. Your instructor will guide you through the stages of writing this paper: selecting a topic, locating sources of information, taking notes, organizing your ideas, writing a rough draft, documenting your sources, and preparing a list of works cited. A well-written research paper will be evidence of your maturity as a writer. Chapters Three and Four of this handbook deal with the writing of a documented essay while Chapter Four deals specifically with literary analysis.

As in English 1021, your instructor will assume that you have mastered Standard English grammar and usage. You will be expected to attend class regularly, to hand in all assignments when they are due, and to avoid plagiarism, a subject discussed thoroughly in Chapter Three: The Documented Essay. It is the policy of Century College that students who are guilty of deliberate plagiarism risk failure for the given work and the course.

The Writing Center

In most sections of English 0080, 0090, and 1021, you are **required** to spend an average of one hour a week in the **Writing Center (Room 3370 West)**. This hour comprises the fourth credit hour for students in sections that meet only three hours per week in the classroom. Many successful composition students do all of their writing assignments in the Writing Center. The Writing Center Coordinator, English instructors, and student consultants work in the Writing Center throughout the day to help you with your writing. See the postings at the Writing Center for current hours of operation.

How to Use the Writing Center

Our mission is to provide an encouraging environment where writers from all disciplines come together for mutual support and assistance with invention, drafting, revision, and editing. Students in most day sections of English 0080, 0090, and 1021 are required to spend 750 minutes in the Writing Center each semester, but you should check your instructor's syllabus for her/his specific requirements.

The Writing Center is open to all Century College students. All services are available on a first come, first served basis only.

The Online Writing Center is another option for students to get assistance with and feedback on their writing and earn credit as part of their required 750 minutes. You may ask general and specific questions about your writing assignments for all of your courses; you may schedule an appointment with participating English Department faculty to discuss your work in a "chat" environment; you may consult links addressing a range of academic writing topics such as documented essays; you may view grammar mini-lectures; and much more. For information on how to register for and use the Online Writing Center, see current handouts located in the Writing Center.

What to bring with you to the Writing Center:

You will need to bring several items with you to the Writing Center in order to receive the best possible help on your writing assignments.

1) **Enough <u>writing-related work</u>** for the amount of time you plan to spend in the Writing Center on that particular day.

2) **The syllabus for your course and any assignment instructions** you received.

3) **Your book and notes from your course**.

4) **Any previous assignments** that show areas in which you might need help.

5) **Paper and a writing utensil**.

6) **A data storage device** for saving the work you do on the computer. **The Writing Center currently recommends the use of USB drives (also known as "flash," "jump," or "pen" drives).** You may also currently use CDs or your portal account for saving your work in the Writing Center. We have three external floppy disk drives available on a first come, first served basis only. For your convenience, please plan to purchase a USB drive.

7) **Your Century Direct portal account information,** including your ID and PIN numbers. If you have not activated your account, you may do so in the Computer Center (W1320-1332).

8) **Specific questions** about your assignments.

What to do when you come to the Writing Center:

1) **Sign in at one of the two computers labeled "Time Log Only" using your student (tech.) ID number.** These log-in computers will record the number of minutes you spend in the Writing Center. These computers do not have any other programs on them, so if you want to type or print, you will need to move to another computer.

2) **Work on <u>writing-related assignments</u> only. (See "What to work on while you are in the Writing Center" below for a list of acceptable <u>writing-related activities</u>.)** If you are not working on a <u>writing-related assignment</u>, you will be asked once to do so. If you continue to work on unrelated material, you will be asked to leave for the day.

3) **If you need help, approach any of the Writing Center consultants and ask them to help you.** Consultants include

the Writing Center Coordinator, English instructors, and student tutors. They are usually at the front of the room at either the table labeled "Instructors' Table" or at the main desk. Currently, the Writing Center offers walk-in help on a first come, first served basis only. You may also make an appointment to use the Online Writing Center

4) **Ask specific questions. (Do not ask consultants to proofread.)** The Writing Center staff **can** answer any questions/concerns related to the overall structure of your paper (for example, whether the paper has a clear thesis statement, etc.). In regards to grammar, there are a few things we can do. We will look at any specific questions you may have. We can also look at a portion of your paper, tell you what types of errors we see, and show you how to fix them; **however, Writing Center consultants will not proofread.** This means that we will not read through your paper in order to find every error that you might have made.

5) **If you wish to work on a draft and do not need a computer, you may work at any of the tables in the Writing Center.**

6) **If you need to use a computer, move to an open workstation.** You will need your Century Direct portal account user name and password in order to log in. There is no waiting list for computer use; however, **computer availability is extremely limited**, especially during peak hours. Students working on coursework are given priority in all Century College labs. Additionally, while using the Writing Center computers, you must be working on a writing-related assignment.

7) **Once you have logged into the computer with your Century Direct portal account user name and password, you will be able to print.** Please be cautious with your paper use. If you need to print from the Internet, copy and paste the desired text into a Word document. **Use a photocopier for making multiple copies.**

8) **Answer politely when consultants ask you to explain what you are working on.** Because many students using the

Writing Center (especially those in English 0080, 0090, and 1021) receive credit for time spent in the Writing Center and because of limited space, **consultants will make sure that students using the Writing Center are working on <u>writing-related assignments</u>.** This means that you may be asked to show the assignment instructions for your work.

9) **When you are ready to leave, log out of the computer you were using AND the Time Log Computer** in order to get credit for the time you spent in the Writing Center.

What to work on while you are in the Writing Center:

The following is a list of acceptable Writing Center activities. If you are not working on a <u>writing-related assignment</u> from this list, you will be asked <u>once</u> to do so. If you continue to work on unrelated material, you will be asked to leave for the day. If you have any questions, please see the Writing Center Coordinator.

1) **Work on any English 0080, 0090, or 1021 course assignments,** including reading for these courses or grammar exercises.

2) **Work on any papers**, including history research papers, English essays, or reflections for any class.

3) **Work on any Grammar practice exercises (including online versions) or grammar issues** you might have.

4) **ONLY work on reading if there is a specific <u>writing-related assignment</u> dependent on the reading**. Be prepared to show consultants the assignment instructions in writing.

5) **Research (including Internet research) for any papers** that you may need to write.

6) **Work with a consultant** on any papers you are assigned.

7) **QUIETLY work with a peer on <u>writing-related assignments</u>** from any class.

8) **Word process** your papers and print them.

9) **Practice typing/word processing** using the software tutorials provided.

Writing Center Rules:

1) **To get credit, you must work on writing.** You must work on a specific <u>writing-related assignment</u> while you are in the Writing Center. For instance, you may work on a paper for your nursing class, but you cannot just read your nursing textbook. If you are reading in preparation for a writing assignment, you may be asked to explain that assignment or to show the assignment instructions.

2) **Non-writing-related homework is <u>not</u> allowed.** Because you are receiving class credit and because of space constraints, you may **not** do homework that does not have a writing-related assignment connected to it.

3) **Remain in the Writing Center while signed in.** If you sign into the Time Log Computers, you must be in the Writing Center. You may **not** go to the Computer Center, Library, etc. **The Writing Center staff randomly checks attendance.** If you are signed in but not present, your minutes for that day will be deleted and other academic dishonesty policies may apply. (See your instructor's syllabus for more details.)

4) **Be courteous to Writing Center consultants and other students using the lab.** Students exhibiting inappropriate behavior will be asked to leave the Writing Center.

5) **Cell phone use is <u>NOT</u> allowed.** This includes text messages, email, games, etc. If you must take a call, put your phone on vibrate or silent and take the phone into the hallway. Please be aware that if the call will take a long time, you should sign out so that you are not marked absent.

6) **Food and beverages are <u>not</u> allowed at the computers.**

7) **We are <u>unable</u> to accommodate children in the Writing Center.** Parents must make other childcare arrangements when planning to use the Writing Center.

8) **Group work is allowed as long as you are quietly working on a <u>writing-related assignment</u>.**

9) **You may listen to music using headphones, but the volume should be turned down** out of respect for the other students using the Writing Center.

10) **Surfing the Internet is not allowed.** This includes all email, video, and websites not related to a <u>specific writing assignment</u> (i.e., Facebook, MySpace, YouTube, etc.).

Resources:

The following resources are available for use in the Writing Center. **All materials must stay in the Writing Center.**

1) **Nineteen computers with Microsoft Office Suite.**

2) **Grammar and keyboarding practice software**.

3) **Printer access.** (Although you will need to log in using your Century Direct portal account in order to print, there is no charge for printer use.)

4) **A variety of handbooks, textbooks, dictionaries, etc**.

5) **Grammar practice exercises with answer keys.**

6) **Internet access, including library catalog access and access to the following recommended websites:**

Century Writing Center:
http://www.century.mnscu.edu/englishdept/writcent.aspx
(With links to many more useful sites!)

Purdue University:
http://owl.english.purdue.edu

ESL Café:
http://www.eslcafe.com

ESLbee.com:
http://eslbee.com

St. Cloud State:
http://leo.stcloudstate.edu

A Writer's Reference:
http://dianahacker.com/writersref/

Grammar Bytes!:
http://www.chompchomp.com

Tips for getting the most out of your Writing Center time:

1) **Start early.** By the end of the semester, the Writing Center begins to get extremely crowded, so it's best to start working on your Writing Center minutes right away. Additionally, the Writing Center is busiest between 9:00 AM and 2:00 PM.

2) **Spend the same amount of time in the Writing Center each week. Unless your instructor has a specific completion requirement,** the Writing Center recommends that you spend at least 50 minutes each week in the Writing Center rather than visiting in one or two long segments. **(Check your instructor's syllabus for specific requirements.)** If you choose to spend a large block of time in the Writing Center, please note that you will still be required to work on writing-related material, regardless of whether you have finished your work for your 0080, 0090, or 1021 course.

3) **Ask specific questions.** Do not ask consultants to "proofread," "look over," or "read through" your paper. Instead, think of some specific sentences that concern you or a particular concept that you find confusing.

   For example:
   "Do my topic sentences support my thesis?"

"Did I use the right word here?"
"Is this sentence a fragment?"
"Can you explain how I might organize a comparison
and contrast paper?"
"Can you show me an example of a process paper?"

4) **Give yourself enough time.** Allow sufficient time after your visit to the Writing Center to revise and edit your work before submitting it to your instructor.

5) **The Writing Center is not a library, so it can be noisy at times.** It is also not a study hall; it is a place to address writing issues.

6) **Consultants are available to offer advice and help.** Meet with them regularly; however, in the final analysis, you are responsible not only for your own work but for the grade you receive.

Remember, the Writing Center's resources are open for use by any Century College student working on any writing project for any class. We hope that you will visit the Writing Center often and that you will continue to use this valuable resource throughout your career at Century College.

1021 Test-Out Procedure

After registering for English 1021, if you feel you are a proficient enough writer to test out of the class, speak directly with your instructor. You may test out of English 1021 only by successfully completing the following procedure.

You will have *two hours* to write a two-page (600–700 words, minimum) essay on a topic chosen by your instructor. The final draft should be typed, double spaced, and formatted with one-inch margins on the top, sides, and bottom. You will take the test under supervision, such as in the Writing Center or an instructor's office, and you may use a computer to write the essay. Three different English 1021 instructors will evaluate the essay based on the following criteria:

- A clear and precise thesis
- Logical organization, with a discernible beginning, middle, and end
- Unity, coherence, and emphasis
- Well-developed paragraphs
- Well-constructed sentences
- No run-on sentences, sentence fragments, or comma splices
- Effective word choice
- Few mechanical errors, including errors in spelling, punctuation, and neatness
- Lively and interesting details and descriptions

If your essay receives a grade of "A" from **each** of the three evaluators, you will be exempted from all further requirements in English 1021. You will receive an "A" for your final grade in the course for which you have registered.

Chapter Two: Writing Basics

Although each composition class has its own instructor, textbook, and assignments, there are a few fundamental guidelines that will be helpful to you. This chapter will cover some basics that apply to writing papers at the college level.

Formatting the Paper

You will be able to communicate more effectively with any audience if your paper is neat and readable. Therefore, it is important that you follow some general format rules. *If your instructor has alternate preferences, follow those rules first.*

- Type or print your paper on standard 8½ by 11-inch unlined paper. Staple or paper-clip all pages together.

- Use only one side of the paper. Double space and leave ample margins of at least one inch on the top, the bottom, and both sides.

- If your instructor allows you to handwrite your papers, write legibly in pen, and follow the guidelines listed above.

- Hand in neat papers. Avoid crossed-out words, erasures, wrinkled pages, and spill marks.

- Center the title at the top of the first page.

- Place page numbers in Arabic numerals (2, 3, 4) in the upper-right-hand corner, beginning with the second page. If you are following MLA format, include your last name alongside the page number in the upper-right-hand corner.

- The heading should include your name, the instructor's name, the course and section numbers, and the due date.

For example:

Stanley Kowalski
Instructor DuBois
English 1021.04
30 Sept. 2007

Essay Assignments

During the course of your work at Century, you will write a variety of essays. Much of the writing you will do, though, will be *expository writing*. Expository writing is directed toward explaining subjects; it is non-fiction and always written with an easily-identified purpose. With few exceptions, the third person point of view ("he/she/they/one/it") is preferred in expository writing rather than first person ("I") or second person ("you").

Depending on the instructor, you might be assigned any of the following: essays using one of several rhetorical modes, a series of persuasive essays, specific writing tasks, a writing portfolio, or documented essays. Each of these is briefly described below. Although the following section *generally* describes typical writing assignments, your instructor will have more specific guidelines for your essays. **Follow the guidelines given by your instructor first**, but consult these definitions if you need more explanation. It is important to note that this list of common essay assignments is not meant to be exhaustive; that is, your instructor may assign writing forms not covered in this section.

Rhetorical modes are expository essays that vary in form, depending on the type of mode. A **narrative** paper, for example, tells a story of something that has happened, relating that event from beginning to end. It should always be focused on a limited series of events or on just one event. A **compare and contrast**, on the other hand, discusses similarities and differences of two or more items in a meaningful manner, whereas a **process analysis** paper explains how to do something or how something is done. Process analysis achieves this goal by detailing the steps necessary to complete a certain task or activity. A **descriptive** essay relates in great detail the characteristics of a person, place, or idea, and an

analysis paper provides a better understanding of the topic by examining its parts or features. Analysis essays are frequently assigned in English 1022.

A very common type of writing assignment is a **persuasion, argument,** or **opinion** paper. These essays will require you to take a position and either defend it or try to persuade your audience to agree with you. The crucial thing to do in these papers is to make your point clear from the beginning. You should anticipate arguments against your position and respond to them. A good persuasive/opinion paper stays focused on its topic and uses solid reasoning with evidence that supports its thesis. Some instructors assign only argument papers in their classes instead of assigning papers using a variety of rhetorical modes during the semester.

Next, a **writing task** assignment is based not on rhetorical mode but on the function or purpose of the piece. Common writing tasks include proposals, letters, autobiographies, job applications, requests for information, and other everyday types of writing. Writing tasks may involve one or more rhetorical modes, such as a proposal to a school board to ban the sales of sweetened sodas and energy drinks from district vending machines. This proposal would incorporate elements of effective persuasive writing and may also analyze the costs to student health by allowing the sale of sweetened drinks at school.

Some instructors may ask you to develop a **writing portfolio** over the course of the semester. A writing portfolio is a collection of completed assignments accompanied by short written narratives in which you discuss the strengths of each piece and your rationale for including it in the portfolio. This commentary is just as important—if not more so—than the essays contained in the portfolio. Portfolios may be hard copies turned in to your instructor, or they may be submitted online through Desire2Learn (D2L), depending on your instructor's preferences. Knowing how to develop effective writing portfolios is a good skill to have because they are sometimes requested as part of scholarship or job applications.

Finally, a **documented essay** might be required as a component of any of the previous assignment types. For example, you could be asked to write a documented analysis or include a documented persuasive paper as part of a larger writing portfolio. A documented essay is one that uses outside resources, either as the topic of research or as supporting details for the main point. Chapter Three discusses in more detail the components and the formatting of a well-written documented essay.

Collaborative Writing/Peer Critique

Sometimes a writing assignment will require group work or peer editing with other members of your class. The activities required for these tasks should not be taken as permission to copy from the work of your classmates. **Collaborative writing** and **peer critique** are two forms of cooperation that are useful resources for a composition class.

Collaborative Writing, also called "joint effort," "writing circle," "writing group," or "constructive help," involves working with other students to suggest topics; write sentences; construct paragraphs; or experiment with words, sentences, and paragraphs. In other words, collaborative writing is an effective way of learning and is far removed from plagiarism.

Peer Critique is a form of collaboration that takes place after you have completed a substantial part or a complete draft of your writing assignment. In a peer critique session, a small group of your fellow students will help you revise your writing, and you will help them revise theirs. If you're looking for the right word, for example, another student can often make a useful suggestion. Peer critique can be a valuable way to share writing experience and to practice the editing skills that you must master if you are to become an effective writer.

Additional Resources

You will need to use a variety of resources when writing a paper. Whether you need to do research or use a word processor, Century College offers access to computers and materials that will assist you in your assignments.

In addition to the Writing Center, the following resources may also prove valuable.

The Computer Center, Room 1320 West, provides software and printer access for all Century College students. Rewriting is easier with a computer because you can insert changes and corrections without rewriting or retyping the whole manuscript.

The Century College Library is located in Room 2264 West and Room 1651 East. Its databases can also be accessed directly at www.century.edu from the Century College homepage.

The Rhetorical Situation

Every writer begins with a subject, a purpose for writing, and an audience to keep in mind as she or he crafts an essay. Effective writers react to the rhetorical situation by making conscious choices about approach, point of view, voice, diction, tone, development strategies, and organization in order to communicate with their audience.

The subject may have been assigned by an instructor or chosen by the writer. Either way, a competent writer will think of ways to develop her or his ideas about it, determine the writing's purpose by reading the assignment carefully and consulting the instructor, and analyze the audience and the audience's needs as readers. For example, if you have been given a writing assignment that calls for academic writing in a college course, you will want to select a topic that is appropriate for college-level writing and to discuss your ideas using language and a point of view that are appropriate for communicating about that topic with a college instructor and your colleagues in the classroom.

All writers have an individual, authentic writing voice that is theirs alone. This voice is what makes an essay a lively, interesting reading experience—decisions about word choice, tone, and sentence structure reflect not only a writer's ideas but the writer as well. Keep in mind that writing is communication, and good communication is an exchange between individuals. Think about ways to use your own, authentic voice to create an original, engaging essay your instructors and classroom colleagues will enjoy reading.

Appropriate **Point of View** is an important aspect in any writing. Following is a brief description of the three perspectives.

First Person ("I"): The first person is useful for personal narrative and some other (generally) less formal academic writing.

Second Person ("You"): The second person is infrequently used but can be appropriate for some writing situations, such as an informational process analysis essay or other writing in which addressing the audience directly is effective.

Third Person ("He/She/It/One/They"): Third person is the most commonly used perspective for formal, academic writing.

Choosing a Topic

Although many instructors will assign a topic for the required papers, sometimes you may have to generate a topic on your own, whether for an opinion paper, a compare/contrast essay, or a documented paper. If you are allowed to choose your own topic, the following suggestions might help you.

    ⅄   **List your interests and relate them to your courses.**

       — Photography
          1. Effects of color photography in advertising (psychology)
          2. Matthew Brady, photographer of the Civil War (history)

   3. Comparisons of photographs and literary portraits
      (literature)

— Sports
   1. The use of drugs by professional athletes (health)
   2. The characteristics of sports heroes in stories and
      plays (literature)
   3. Choice of leisure time activities and social class
      (sociology)

— Lifestyles
   1. American writers in Paris in the 1920s (literature)
   2. Changing patterns of energy use and production
      (science)
   3. Marriage in another culture (anthropology)

⋏ **Browse through textbooks and class notes from any of
your classes. Ask questions about facts you've learned.**

— What led to a certain event?
— Why did a certain historical or literary character act the
  way he or she did?
— What effect did a historical event have on the future?
— Is there any relationship between two events?
— How is "A" like or unlike "B"?

⋏ **Look through magazines and journals in the field
about which you have chosen to write. The articles
will give you ideas for a topic and probably help with
some resource ideas.**

⋏ **Examine encyclopedias and dictionaries in the field.
Use these for overviews of the topic, not as primary or
secondary sources.**

⋏ **Avoid the following topics:**

— Highly technical, learned, or specialized topics.
— Topics about which there is not very much research
  material, such as overly current events or non-
  disputed subjects.

— Highly controversial or emotionally charged topics like abortion or gun control, unless you can find and objectively analyze sources on all sides of the issue.
— Subjects that are common topics of debate or that have had quite a bit written about them already.

Restricting the Topic

An important part of thinking about a paper topic—research or otherwise—is restricting a general topic to one that can be developed in the required number of pages. Listed below are two broad topics that have been narrowed and then expressed as thesis statements.

Broad topic:	Robots
Topic:	Robots in science fiction
Restricted Topic:	Robots in the science fiction of Isaac Asimov
Narrower Topic:	The language of Asimov's robots
Thesis:	In portraying robots that can use language as well as humans, Isaac Asimov oversimplifies the problem of designing machines to speak human languages.

Broad Topic:	Relationships
Topic:	Traditional marriage relationships
Restricted Topic:	Traditional marriage customs in South American cultures
Narrower Topic:	Marriage customs in rural Peru
Thesis:	Marriage customs in Peru have evolved from a combination of religious, historical, and geographical influences.

Essay Structure

As an experienced reader and writer, you know that essays will be comprised of three main sections: an introduction, a body, and a conclusion.

The introduction paragraph(s) establishes the topic and focus of your essay, supplying context and creating interest, and usually states your thesis. There are many ways to begin an essay including sharing an anecdote (a small story), describing a scene, making a surprising statement, asking a question, presenting a fact or statistic, and so on.

The body supports and develops the thesis in a series of paragraphs. There is no absolute rule about how many paragraphs the body (or for that matter, the entire essay) must contain. However, most body sections typically will feature at least three paragraphs. Each paragraph should be well developed and coherent so that a reader can readily follow the various points offered in support of the thesis.

The conclusion reinforces the thesis and brings a sense of completeness to the essay. This might be done by reviewing key points, looking to the future, presenting a final detail or example that illustrates the thesis, and so on.

Writing Thesis Statements

A thesis statement (sometimes called a controlling idea) is a sentence stating the central idea that you will be developing in your essay. It is important to remember that the thesis is your own idea; it is the main idea you have come to based upon your experiences, your research, and/or your reading.

Your thesis statement gives direction and structure to your paper. Every part of your paper must support your thesis statement. Ideas irrelevant to your thesis, no matter how interesting they may be, destroy the unity of your paper and thereby confuse your readers.

You may discover your preliminary thesis as you brainstorm or after you write a first draft. While writing the drafts of your paper, you may make changes in your thesis to include new ideas that have occurred to you. Your thesis appears in its final form in the final draft of your essay, usually in the introduction—though it is rarely the first sentence. Even if your thesis is not explicitly stated, you should know what it is and be able to explain it. Occasionally a thesis may be stated at the end of an essay.

A thesis should do the following:
- Identify and limit the topic
- Make an assertion about the topic—a statement that must be elaborated and supported
- Make a third-person, objective statement—never a subjective "I feel that..." or "to me...."
- Present a claim that will not simply be regarded as fact by a majority of readers

Examples of Thesis Statements:

- **Topic of search: The river as symbol in <u>Huck Finn</u>**

  The Mississippi River becomes a symbol of freedom.

  The river, symbolic of natural purity and freedom, contrasts to the shore, symbolic of society's restrictions and corruption.

  The river, although a symbol of freedom throughout much of <u>Huck Finn</u>, is finally powerless to deliver the freedom it symbolizes.

  Mark Twain uses the river to symbolize freedom by emphasizing its remoteness, its power, and its natural richness.

  The river in <u>Huck Finn</u> symbolizes three themes: escape, power, and freedom.

- **Topic of search: Pros and cons of school uniforms**

School uniforms may detract from individuality but are helpful in creating a sense of group identity and school pride.

School uniforms violate the First Amendment right of expression and are not proven to have an effect on student behavior.

School uniforms are a simple method of combating gang violence, crime, and dangerous behavior on school grounds.

The benefits of school uniforms are convenience, security, and affordability.

Creating an Outline

An outline is a step-by-step layout or map of how you are going to write your paper. You will want to have constructed your thesis statement and include it directly in the outline. You may also want to have an idea of your topic sentences for each paragraph. *Outlines can vary in formality,* so if your instructor requires you to turn in an outline, be sure to have him or her explain how detailed it needs to be.

Sample Outline

I.   Thesis Statement:

Witnessing Hurricane Erin was a fascinating yet frightening experience.

     Supporting Detail:

          A. Early interest and ignorance

          B. A rough ride

          C. The aftermath

II.   Topic Sentence:

Ignorant of the terrifying power the relatively small hurricane possessed, I was looking forward to the encounter.

     Supporting Detail:

          A. Past interest

          B. Watching the first half

          C. Was that it?

III.   Topic Sentence:

The eye of the hurricane was a beautifully tranquil sight that lasted nearly forty-five minutes, but the calm quickly turned to chaos.

     Supporting Detail:

          A. Underestimating Erin

          B. Becoming increasingly nervous

          C. Erin finally moves on

A Sample Essay

Because you will be writing many different types of papers in your composition classes, it may be helpful to look at the general structure of a good essay. The following narrative paper was written for English 1021.

Brad Edwards   Edwards 1

Mr. Bill Matthews

English 1021.23

7 Feb. 2007

Erin's Wrath

On August 3, 1995, an ominous presence was heading toward the Florida panhandle city of Pensacola: a single-eyed, whirling monstrosity called Hurricane Erin. She had been gaining strength and was moving north along the Gulf of Mexico after roaring across southern Florida. My brother Mark, his wife Kristi, and I were anxiously watching the weather channel for updates because our house was about five miles from the Gulf, just north of Pensacola. All the weather reports stated that the storm would make landfall around noon, but by 8:00 a.m., an eerie quiet had enveloped the neighborhood. Hurricane Erin was coming, and there was nothing anybody could do about it. By the end of the day, I would find my experience to be both fascinating and frightening.

Ignorant of the terrifying power the relatively small hurricane possessed, I was looking forward to the encounter. I grew up in the Midwest loving thunderstorms. The flash of lightning, booming thunder, and hailstorms were all things I thought were pretty cool. So at 11:30 a.m., I decided to grab a seat on the porch bench and watch the show. What struck me first was the sky. Wide bands of gray-white clouds marched ever closer, like a colossal army stretched across the horizon. Within a few minutes, the bands had merged to form a solid blanket of gray with no definition, encompassing the whole sky. Then came the wind and rain. It started as a whisper, but with each passing minute, the velocity seemed to double until it began to howl at a constant speed. Every tree in the neighborhood was leaning at a thirty-degree angle as if trying to hide from the onslaught. A group of about ten, forty-foot tall pine trees were groaning and creaking their protests at the violent, relentless gale. Small pieces of debris were made into hurling projectiles by the fierce wind. The rain appeared to be falling sideways into the porch, but I was fairly protected by the house, so I wasn't too concerned for my safety yet and continued to watch the spectacle. The hour and a half barrage seemed to last much longer than that, but just as quickly as the storm developed, it was gone. One minute driving wind and rain and the next sunshine and blue sky surrounded me. It took a moment to figure out what had happened, but I soon realized I was in the eye of a hurricane!

The eye of Hurricane Erin was a beautifully tranquil sight that lasted nearly forty-five minutes, but the calm quickly turned to chaos. As before, I saw a huge wall of clouds pushing its way into the fleeting sunlight. From what I remembered about hurricanes, the wind in the bottom half blows in the opposite direction as the top half. What I forgot was that the wind is also much more powerful. I was instantly struck in the face by a burst of wind-driven sand and rain. The force was so great it nearly knocked me over. My fascination with Erin had abruptly ended and was replaced by a growing sense of fear. I scrambled into the house to looks of disapproval and "I told you so" from my brother and sister-in-law. By this time, the electricity had been knocked out, so we sat in the stale, warming air of the living room, listening to the sounds of Erin's wrath and not saying a word. The earlier groaning and creaking of the trees were now punctuated by loud cracks, clearly heard inside the house. The wail of the wind crescendoed into a high-pitched scream that sent chills through my bones. An hour later, the scream at long last subsided to a loud murmur. Finally, after nearly four hours of fury, Erin's anger was directed elsewhere.

As I opened the door, the storm's destructive power was fully revealed. Almost all of the tall pine trees had been snapped in half as though they had been made of toothpicks. Majestic oak trees were uprooted as if a giant had pulled them like weeds. Our beloved basketball hoop, including the ten-foot pole and concrete base, lay in a tangled heap next to a fallen tree. A gaping hole marked the spot where it had once proudly stood. A neighbor's boat had been flipped on its side like a discarded bathtub toy. Leaves, branches, paper, and basically anything that hadn't been secured covered the ground like a blanket. Part of the siding on the house was ripped off, along with a few shingles, but it seemed as if most of the damage had been done to the trees. I wanted to check out the rest of the neighborhood but soon discovered that huge trees had toppled across every road leading out.

The lingering effects of Erin would last for days. Grocery stores ran out of food, gas stations couldn't pump gas, and no traffic lights made driving totally crazy. Most power was returned in two days, but our power wasn't restored until five days after the storm. During those five days, the house became a sauna, sleeping was impossible, showers had no hot water, our refrigerator was a 48-quart cooler, and I made up for about three years of reading inactivity. Erin was officially labeled a Category 1 hurricane, the smallest in a scale of one to five, with sustained winds of 95 mph and gusts up to 110 mph. Four storm-related deaths were reported along with $700 million in damage. A seven-foot wall of water slammed into Pensacola Beach, destroying the fishing pier and leaving the once rolling dunes flat and featureless.

I am confident in saying that anyone who encounters a hurricane will have an incredible amount of respect for the awesome power of nature. What I remember most about the experience was my fascination with the storm's unyielding power, the damage, and the intense moments of fear that power caused. Hopefully, this was a once-in-a-lifetime exposure to the wrath of a hurricane, but there is no doubt that Hurricane Erin has left an indelible mark upon my memory.

Evaluating the Essay

The final form of good expository writing is determined by the writer's subject, purpose, and audience. For example, an essay on saturated fats addressed to an audience of nutritionists will be quite different from an essay on the same topic addressed to an audience of people who want to lose weight. Nevertheless, all good expository writing shares some common features. The goal of your instructors, no matter the course, is to help you write papers with these characteristics:

- A clear and precise thesis
- Logical organization, with a discernible beginning, middle, and end
- Unity, coherence, and emphasis
- Well-developed paragraphs
- Well-constructed sentences
- No run-on sentences, sentence fragments, or comma splices
- Effective word choice
- Few mechanical errors, including errors in spelling, punctuation, and neatness
- Lively and interesting details and descriptions

Your instructor may elaborate upon these standards.

Common Errors in Writing

The following is a list of common errors and trouble spots that English instructors find in student writing. It is designed to help you both avoid and correct such errors in your own written work.

For each error below, you will find a definition, an example with one or more errors, and a sample correction. Errors are indicated in boldface in the examples, while corrections are marked with bold and underlining.

PLEASE NOTE: There may be more than one way to correct these errors, and we suggest you consult a reliable grammar guide or your instructor for guidance on alternatives. For more information or practice worksheets on these topics, stop by the Writing Center on campus or consult the Writing Center's website.

Apostrophe errors: Apostrophes are used to indicate possession in nouns, mark left out letters in contractions, and help to distinguish between "its/it's." Errors in possession often occur when the writer omits the apostrophe or uses it in the wrong place in the word. Errors with plurals and contractions are also common.

Example with error: *The campus gaming **groups** meetings take place every Wednesday evening. The old meeting location changed **it's** hours of operation, so **theyll** have to move the meetings to the student union.*

Possessive nouns in English are formed by adding an apostrophe and the letter "s" ('s). All possessive nouns require an apostrophe. The most common error with apostrophes involves plural possessive nouns. Here, the apostrophe comes after the plural ending.

Correction: *The campus gaming **groups'** meetings take place every Wednesday evening. The old meeting location changed **its** hours of operation, so **they'll** have to move the meetings to the student union.*

Clichés: Clichés are expressions that are extremely familiar to most people. For that reason, they are easy to use. Unfortunately, the overuse of such expressions causes them to lose all impact in academic writing. Avoid using clichés.

Example with error: *Because Marcus had so much to do on Saturday before leaving on vacation, he woke up at* **the crack of dawn**.

The expression "the crack of dawn" is a cliché. Avoiding clichés is as simple as finding an alternate way to express the idea.

Correction: *Because Marcus had so much to do on Saturday before leaving for vacation, he woke up* **much earlier than usual**.

Comma splice: A comma splice occurs when a writer incorrectly combines two or more sentences (independent clauses) with only a comma.

Example with error: *It was a sunny day, the students asked if class could be held outside.*

There are various methods to correct a comma splice. These include using a comma with a coordinating conjunction, breaking it into two sentences, replacing the comma with a semicolon (;), or rephrasing the sentence. Two possible corrections are shown below.

Correction: *It was a sunny day; the students asked if class could be held outside.* **Or** *It was a sunny day,* **so** *the students asked if class could be held outside.*

Comma errors: Commas have many uses in English. They separate items in a series, set off introductory phrases and asides from the rest of the sentence, and connect clauses when used with joining words. Commas are also used in quotations, dates, addresses, numbers, and professional titles.

Example with error: *"This week we will cover commas apostrophes semicolons and colons in class" said the instructor. "The quiz coming up on November 1 2007 will cover all these areas."*

Any good grammar or writing textbook can help you identify when to use commas appropriately. There are also many resources available in the Writing Center.

Correction: *"This week we will cover commas, apostrophes, semicolons, and colons in class,"* said the instructor. *"The quiz coming up on November 1, 2007, will cover all these areas."*

Leaving out a comma can sometimes dramatically change the meaning of a sentence—usually not for the better. Consider the following example with error:

The program's target audience includes the following groups: pregnant women, low-income families, single adults without **children and caretakers.**

Because the writer has neglected to put a comma after "children," the last phrase of the sentence means that one of the program's target audiences is single adults without children AND without caretakers. The term "caretakers" becomes part of the prepositional phrase started by "without." The omitted comma has created a meaning other than what the writer intended.

Correction: *The program's target audience includes the following groups: pregnant women, low-income families, single adults without* **children, and caretakers.**

Dangling or misplaced modifier: A misplaced modifier is separated from the word or phrase it modifies, as in the following example.

Example with error: ***Sleeping during the lecture,*** *the instructor marked me absent.*

It is not the instructor who is sleeping but the student speaking the sentence; therefore, the sentence needs to be reworded. Dangling modifiers can often be corrected by rewording.

Correction: ***Because I was sleeping*** *during the lecture, the instructor marked me absent.*

Double negatives: English almost always requires a single term to indicate negatives. Using two or more negatives is incorrect.

Example with error: *We **don't** have **no** papers in Biology 1020 this semester.*

To correct a double negative, eliminate one of the negative terms.

Correction: *"We **don't** have **any** papers in Biology 1020 this semester."*

I vs. me: Pronouns can function three ways in a sentence: as a subject, an object, or a marker of possession. The form of each pronoun varies depending on the function it assumes. This can create problems for writers who are not sure of the roles subject, object, and possessive markers fulfill in a sentence. As a result, there is confusion over which to use, especially when it comes to the pronouns *I* and *me*.

Example with error: *Mom gave **Tom and I** a list of errands to run for her this afternoon. Do you want to come along with **Lisa and I**?*

In the first sentence, the pronoun should be in the objective form (me), as it is the object of the verb "gave." In the second sentence, the first pronoun follows a preposition, and therefore should be in objective form as well.

This can be a confusing topic. For more advice and examples on when to use "I" vs. "me," consult a good grammar guide or visit the Writing Center or the Writing Center website.

Correction: *Mom gave **Tom and me** a list of errands to run for her this afternoon. Do you want to come along with **Lisa and me?***

Parallelism errors: Whenever a list or series of terms occurs within a sentence, those terms need to be in the same grammatical form. This is called *parallel construction*. Failing to do this is called a lack of parallelism.

Example with error: *I like movies, old television shows, and* **reading comic books**.

In this example, the phrase "reading comic books" is not a parallel construction. It contains a participle (reading), whereas the other two elements are simply nouns. To correct a lack of parallelism, change all items in the series to the same part of speech. Notice how the corrected sentence does this.

Correction: *I like movies, old television shows, and* **comic books**.

Person shift: A person shift occurs when a writer changes the point of view in his or her writing (from third to second, for example, as shown).

Example with error: *Students can take advantage of the many resources in the Writing Center.* **You** *can use computers to research or work with an instructor.*

Person shifts can be avoided by keeping in mind the audience and purpose. Pick one audience and stick to that for the length of the paper.

Correction: *Students can take advantage of the many resources in the Writing Center.* **They** *can use computers to research or work with an instructor.*

Plurals: Incorrectly formed plurals are becoming more common in written English. The most frequent mistake involves using an apostrophe to form a plural, especially with words ending in a vowel.

Example with error: *We had the best* **taco's** *for dinner at Boca Chica the other night. The* **bus'es** *took the entire band there after the concert.*

Remember: plurals in English **never** require an apostrophe. See the section on apostrophes above for help with plural possessives.

Correction: *We had the best **tacos** for dinner at Boca Chica the other night. The **buses** took the entire band there after the concert.*

Preposition misuse: Many verbs in English use prepositions. Errors occur when writers misuse the preposition that usually accompanies a verb. This often creates a prepositional phrase that has no meaning in English.

Example with error: *I love rain when I am in a bad mood; the severe thunderstorm really **cheered me off**. I hope the rain continues to fall **onto** this evening.*

Preventing this kind of error is a matter of checking a reliable dictionary to make sure the preposition you have used is acceptable with that verb.

Correction: *I love rain when I am in a bad mood; the severe thunderstorm really **cheered me up**. I hope the rain continues to fall **into** this evening.*

Prepositions at the end of a sentence: In the past, it was always an error to end a sentence in English with a preposition. English is a language in transition, however, so that rule is not as rigidly followed as it once was. Many prepositions are acceptable to use at the end of a sentence, while some are still incorrect.

Note: Check with your instructor to see if he or she considers it acceptable to use prepositions at the end of a sentence. Some may prefer you to avoid using them this way.

Example with error: *Where are you **at**?*

In this case, the preposition "at" is unnecessary and incorrect, since "where" already asks for a location.

Correction: ***Where are you?***

Pronoun misuse: Pronouns do one of two things: they replace nouns and/or they refer back to nouns. Pronouns must agree in number and type with the nouns to which they refer. Errors occur when writers replace nouns with pronouns that differ either in type or number.

Example with error: *Desperation is **where** students feel they have to cheat. Students **that** plagiarize should face disciplinary measures.*

Although the relative pronoun "that" can refer back to things or people, it is preferable to use it only in relation to things. When referring to a person, give preference to "who" or "whom" instead. Similarly, "where" should be used only to refer to places.

Correction: *Desperation is a feeling **that** drives students to cheat. Students **who** plagiarize should face disciplinary measures.*

Pronoun number shift: As stated above, pronouns must agree in number with the nouns they replace. Changing number (from singular to plural, for example) is incorrect.

Example with error: *The students are going to get **his** research done at the library this weekend. I will do **their** research next week.*

In this example, the noun "students" is plural, whereas the pronoun that refers back to it is singular—"his." In the second sentence, the subject "I" is singular and the pronoun "their" is plural. To avoid these errors, make sure all pronouns reflect the same number as the nouns they refer to or replace.

Correction: *The students are going to get **their** research done at the library this weekend. I will do **my** research next week.*

Punctuation: Every sentence in English needs correct punctuation, both to complete it and to mark important breaks such as pauses or asides. No matter the type of sentence, make sure to use an appropriate punctuation mark to complete it. Errors occur when writers omit punctuation or use punctuation marks incorrectly.

Example with error: *Why would you want to do that. I don't know?*

The type of punctuation used depends on the kind of sentence. When asking a question, use a question mark. When making a simple statement, use a period to end the sentence. Exclamation points are rarely, if ever, used in academic writing. Remember also to use any necessary punctuation within a sentence, such as commas, colons, or semicolons. The Writing Center has many handouts and books that can help you in this area.

Correction: *Why would you want to do that**?** I don't know**.**

Redundancies, including unnecessary repetitions: Any time an idea is repeated or unnecessary information appears in the text, the writer has a redundancy. Redundancies and repetitions often occur when assignments include a word or sentence count requirement and writers struggle to meet that requirement.

Example with error: *The light at sunset was beautiful.* ***The light** shone over the prairie and cast a soft orange light over everything. The **very unique beauty** of the scene was unforgettable.*

To eliminate redundancies in your writing, try combining shorter sentences into one, or use a good dictionary to vary the terms you use.

Correction: *The light at sunset was beautiful **and cast** a soft orange **glow over the prairie**. The **unique charm** of the scene was unforgettable.*

Run-on or fused sentence: A run-on or fused sentence is one in which two or more complete sentences (independent clauses) are joined without any punctuation. As the name implies, these sentences go on and on without any breaks. The result is sometimes a sentence which is very confusing to the reader.

Example with error: *While working on a research paper for a class it is important to make sure you have all your sources accurately documented at the same time make sure to indicate where you cite directly from a source where you paraphrase and where you summarize.*

To correct a run-on or fused sentence, add punctuation such as a semicolon, use a semicolon or comma plus a joining word, or break the sentence into two or more shorter sentences. Notice that the corrected example has added punctuation between the sentences as well as within each sentence.

Correction: *While working on a research paper for a class, it is important to make sure you have all your sources accurately documented. **At** the same time, make sure to indicate where you cite directly from a source, where you paraphrase, and where you summarize.*

Sentence fragment: As its name implies, a sentence fragment is a partial or incomplete sentence. It cannot stand alone and requires another clause or phrase to complete it.

Example with error: ***Whether** you can leave now.*

To fix a sentence fragment, combine it with another sentence (often one that appears before or after the fragment in your paper), or add a clause to complete the thought.

Correction: ***You need to ask your boss** whether you can leave now.*

Spelling errors/lack of proofreading: This kind of error most often occurs when writers use spell-check and grammar-check features instead of manually proofreading.

Example with error: *The last **weak** of the semester is tough on everyone. **Its** important to remind yourself that **the the** end is **near***

Although spell-check and grammar-check features do catch some mistakes, they cannot catch all of them. They will almost always miss incorrectly used homonyms (see Glossary). It is important to read through your draft before turning it in or, better yet, have someone else read your essay to spot errors you might have missed. Look up any word you might have misspelled.

Correction: *The last **week** of the semester is tough on everyone. **It's** important to remind yourself that **the** end is **near.***

Split infinitive: In English, the infinitive form of a verb is treated like one word. Both parts therefore should be kept together ("to go," "to run," "to write," etc.) Generally, inserting an adverb in between the parts of an infinitive is incorrect.

Example with error: *...**to boldly go** (sorry, Trekkies) where no one has gone before.*

To avoid split infinitive errors, re-organize the word order to keep the infinitive phrase together.

Correction: *...**to go boldly** where no one has gone before.*

Subject-verb agreement: The subject and verb of each sentence must agree with each other; that is, a single subject requires a single verb form, and a plural subject requires a plural verb form. Mixing the two is problematic.

Example with error: *The students **goes** to the library each semester to do their research. The librarian **show** them how to use the school's databases to find articles and books.*

To correct subject-verb agreement errors, make sure the conjugated verb matches the subject in number.

Correction: *The students **go** to the library each semester to do their research. The librarian **shows** them how to use the school's databases to find articles and books.*

Vagueness: Vagueness occurs when pronouns are used without a clear antecedent (reference noun).

Example with error: *I don't think **they** should charge so much for cell phone plans.*

In this example, the pronoun "they" is a vague reference. Who exactly is they? Cell phone companies? People who use cell phones? Another group entirely? It is not clear from the sentence as it is written. To correct, make sure pronouns have a clear reference noun.

Correction: *I don't think **cell phone companies** should charge so much for **their** plans.*

Verb conjugation: Conjugation errors, such as subject-verb agreement errors, occur when writers use the wrong verb form. In this case, however, the conjugated verb is not standard English.

Example with error: *What **do** he do for a living? I **does** not know.*

To correct, use the standard English conjugation form. A good grammar book can help you if you get stuck.

Correction: *What **does** he do for a living? I **do** not know.*

Verb tense shift: A verb tense shift (or verb shift) occurs when writers unnecessarily change between verb tenses or times, for example from past to present.

Example with error: *It has been sunny ever since we **are** here.*

To correct, keep verb tenses the same unless details require a shift in time.

Correction: *It has been sunny ever since we **have been** here.*

Voice shift: A voice shift occurs when a writer changes between the active and passive voices in the same sentence. Writers sometimes rely on passive constructions to make their writing sound more sophisticated; in reality, using the passive often makes writing sound confusing or convoluted.

Example with error: ***The home-run ball was caught by a fan*** *in the second row of seats, and everyone in our group was jealous of her good luck.*

It is important to note that passive constructions are rarely the best choice for your essays. Because the active voice brings clarity to writing, choose the active voice whenever you can. For more information on how to spot and correct passive voice constructions in your writing, visit the Writing Center or the Writing Center website.

Correction: **<u>A fan in the second row of seats caught the home-run ball</u>**, and everyone in our group was jealous of her good luck.

Wordiness: Wordy sentences are those which use unnecessary words or neglect to make straightforward, simple statements.

Example with error: *The **building has the essential features of a** cottage, and **it exists** on a bank that extends over the St. Croix.*

To correct, simplify the sentence and be as direct as possible.

Correction: *The **<u>cottage sits</u>** on a bank that extends over the St. Croix.*

Chapter Three:
The Documented Essay

In order to meet one of the goals of English 1021 and 1022, you will write a short (two to five pages) documented essay. In this exercise, you will learn to use outside materials to develop and support your own thesis. This section of the handbook will help you master in-text citations and bibliography form. Most of the techniques used in writing a documented essay are used in 1022 when writing longer literary research papers.

Plagiarism Explained

It goes without saying that the writing you turn in must be your own, not someone else's. Although we encourage collaboration, peer editing, and properly documented summary, paraphrase, and direct quotation, we will not tolerate plagiarism (the unacknowledged use of materials from other sources). Plagiarism includes the use not only of professionally written material but also of papers written by other students.

Let's examine the most serious forms of plagiarism. The first kind is obvious: the plagiarist simply copies a passage word-for-word without mentioning the source. The second kind is just as deceptive: the plagiarist changes a few terms and copies the passage, again without mentioning the source. Another obviously unacceptable form of plagiarism is turning in an entire paper you did not write. If you practice any form of deliberate plagiarism, you will receive an "F" on the plagiarized essay and may fail the entire course.

Examine the following passage from Rachel Carson's *Silent Spring*:

The history of life on earth has been a history of
interaction between living things and their surroundings.
To a large extent, the physical form and the habits of the
earth's vegetation and its animal life have been molded by
the environment. Considering the whole span of earthly
time, the opposite effect, in which life actually modifies its
surroundings, has been relatively slight. Only within the
moment of time represented by the present century has
one species—man—acquired significant power to alter the
nature of his world (16).

Now, let's change a few terms and write a crude paraphrase
without any reference to Rachel Carson or *Silent Spring*.

Life on earth has been a history of encounters between
living beings and their surroundings. The physical form
and habits of both vegetation and animal life have to a
large extent been molded by the environment. Over the
large span of time in the earth's history, the opposite effect
in which life forms change the environment has been
relatively insignificant. Only in the last century has one
species—man—acquired the power to change the nature of
his world.

Using a paragraph like this without reference to Rachel Carson is a serious incidence of plagiarism. Additionally, notice that this paragraph contains several *exact phrases* from the original source with no quotation marks to show that these phrases are identical to the original material.

Life on earth has been a history of encounters **between living** beings **and their surroundings. The physical form and habits** of both vegetation and animal life have **to a large extent** been **molded by the environment**. Over the large span of time in the earth's history, **the opposite effect, in which life** forms change the environment, has been relatively insignificant. Only in the last **century has one species—man—acquired** the **power to** change **the nature of his world**.

These phrases marked in bold are directly lifted from the original text. Thus, even if you *were* to include a citation at the end of the section, *you would still be plagiarizing* because direct quotations *must* have quotation marks around them. Careless paraphrasing such as this results in unintentional plagiarism. In this case, a direct quotation is presented as paraphrase. If you prefer to use a number of well-written phrases from your source material, remember to use quotation marks and to cite your source.

Other common mistakes are misquotation, faulty paraphrase, and the attribution of material to the wrong source. These less serious forms of plagiarism are still deceptive and usually result in an "F" for the paper in which they appear.

The following section on paraphrasing and using quotations will help you to learn how to use the work of other writers legitimately, strengthening support for your own thesis. Plagiarism will not be a problem once you have learned how to integrate the comments of other writers into your own writing.

Paraphrasing, Summarizing, and Using Quotations

The published ideas and opinions of other writers can effectively support your own assertions because they show that well-known authorities share your interpretations. Here are some guidelines to follow when you use borrowed materials:

- Use the comments of recognized authorities as support for your own conclusions. Use quotation marks to enclose direct quotations, that is, sentences with exactly the same wording as the original, and for striking words and phrases from the original.

- Acknowledge all ideas that you borrow from another writer, whether they are directly quoted, summarized, or paraphrased. Paraphrasing is distinguished from summarization by the fact that it simply restates the exact meaning of a short passage in your own words. Summarization selects and condenses the main points of a longer text. Paraphrase is also different from summary in that it should be about the same length as the original text, whereas a summary is significantly shorter. The source of a summary should always be cited, just as a paraphrase would be.

- Use quotations sparingly. Paraphrased or summarized material is easier to incorporate into the structure of your paragraph and to harmonize with your style.

- Never let quotations speak for themselves. Always use quotations in support of your own assertions. If it is not clear how a quotation supports an assertion you have made, you must explain.

- A quotation should never stand alone. You should incorporate quotations smoothly into your own writing by introducing quotations with short explanatory phrases or by using phrases after the quotation to connect it to the following sentence.

⋏ Careful paraphrasing is preferable to a long quotation.

⋏ Place quotations longer than four typewritten lines in a separate block apart from the main text, double-spaced and indented 1 inch from the left margin. Do not enclose these long quotes in quotation marks. (See page 3 of the sample essay for an example of how this should look.)

⋏ Long quotations often include material that does not relate to your point. Use an ellipsis (...) to omit irrelevancies.

⋏ A direct quotation within a direct quotation is indicated by using single quotation marks within double quotation marks: *"She said, 'I don't know,'" he explained.*

⋏ Periods and commas at the end of a quotation always go inside the quotation marks. Colons, semicolons, question marks, and exclamation points go inside the quotation marks when they are part of the quote ("Did she pass the test?" he asked.) and outside when they are part of the sentence in which the quote occurs (Did she say, "I passed the test"?).

Organizing Your Ideas

Once you have narrowed down your topic, considered a thesis statement, and begun research, you will need to decide how to keep track of your information and ideas. Whatever method you choose will probably involve some sort of outline. Outlines can be a valuable tool for drafting essays. They help you to organize your ideas, and they can indicate areas of possible weakness—points that need further development and/or supporting details and examples.

An outline should include your thesis or controlling idea and the main points you want to make. It can help you as you draft your essay by illustrating a possible line of thought or method of development. It helps you illustrate that all claims are related to your topic. As you write, re-write, and revise your essay, your outline may also evolve to reflect these changes.

Some instructors may ask you to include a formal outline (complete sentences, Roman and Arabic numerals, sub-points, and so forth). Some may prefer a modified outline of phrases or even a list or series of statements that indicate key ideas or points of the paper. An outline is your tool, a guideline that helps you remember what ideas need to be included and the most effective arrangement of those ideas—spatial, chronological, or other. One possible format is provided. Instructors differ in their requirements for papers, so be sure to follow the format guidelines of your instructor.

Sample Outline

I. Introduction and Thesis:
There are many benefits of school uniforms, such as convenience, security, and affordability. (Thesis that will be included in the introductory paragraph)

II. Convenience and practicality of school uniforms
(Topic sentence, paragraph one)

A. Simplify choices (Supporting details)
B. Saving time

III. Uniforms to build community
(Topic sentence, paragraph two)

A. Increase community with recognition
B. Improved behavior—community association

IV. Increase security
(Topic sentence, paragraph three)

A. The Long Beach Unified School district statistic
B. Minimizing dangerous influences
    1. Gangs (Supporting details of point B, paragraph three)
    2. Hidden weapons in clothing
    3. No fights over designer clothes

V. Possible negative aspects (Affordability)
(Topic sentence, paragraph four)

A. Karin Polacheck of LBUSD defense ("affordable school uniforms can reduce clothing costs substantially. . . . ")
(Notice how the quotation from notes is included on the outline, showing how that information fits into the paper.)

VI.   Conclusion: benefits outweighing possible drawbacks.
(A short summary statement for the concluding paragraph, relates back to the thesis statement without restating it exactly.)

A Sample Documented Essay

The following documented persuasive essay was written for a 1021 class and is a good model because of its organization, clarity, and strong supporting details. It properly cites outside sources and follows the correct format for spacing and page numbers.

(A possible example of a format precedes the essay. Instructors differ in requirements, so be sure to follow the guidelines of your instructor.)

Ed Slackerr   Slackerr 1

Instructor deSaint

English 1021.65

3 Nov. 2007

The Fine Art of Procrastination

Following the adage of "Don't put off until tomorrow what you can do today" only leads to trouble. Those who want to succeed in

---

Emily Troeger   Troeger 1

Instructor DuBois

English 1021.04

30 Sept. 2007

School Uniforms for Public School Children

When the principal of my high school in Germany made the suggestion of introducing school uniforms into our public school, the majority of students, as well as our parents, voted against it. The school uniforms were only part of his attempt to make our high school one of the superior ones in the area. My friends and I did not like the attitude with which he rushed in and basically told us that everything we liked about our school so far was bad. Additionally, the arrogant way he presented himself did not make us want to listen to his suggestions, let alone accept them. So I, along with many others, voted for individuality and against school uniforms. Today, taking care of three children who attend a private school where uniforms are mandatory, I see many benefits of school uniforms, such as convenience, security, and affordability.

Probably the most obvious benefit of school uniforms is that they are practical and convenient. In the mornings, instead of having to decide whether to wear the purple skirt or the pink pants, the girls choose from among their blue uniform pants. Thus, the process of getting our three children ready in the mornings takes much less time than without uniforms. For example, one of them, Nicholas, just recently switched from a public school to St. Odilia's Catholic School. I monitored the amount of time it took him to get ready for school before and after because I was interested in if and how school uniforms would affect it. His time was cut down from about thirty to fifteen minutes.

Apart from the convenience, school uniforms build a sense of community as well as security. Students can easily recognize each other as belonging to the same school because they are wearing the school colors and symbol. When cheering for a school sports team, the same colors create a "we-belong-together" feeling as well as a sense of unity and school pride. This school pride also helps the children behave when they are not in school. They learn that whatever they do reflects on their school and fellow students, so they act more responsibly in order to keep from shining a bad light on their school. School uniforms help students identify with their school and with each other.

For many parents, the various ways in which school uniforms can increase the children's security are probably the most important reason for considering pro-uniform politics. Studies of the Long Beach Unified School District (LBUSD) found a "drop in school crime in Long Beach, California, since school uniforms were mandated for kindergarteners through eighth-graders in 1994 [of] 86 [percent]" ("Go Figure" 72). There are many possible explanations for this drastic drop in school crime. First of all, visitors can easily be recognized by their clothing, which gives the school staff and the students the opportunity to monitor who belongs to the school; thus, possible dangers from intruders can be prevented. In many public schools gang fights and theft are seen on a daily basis. School uniforms would minimize those aspects that make school dangerous for our children. Gang members are not able to show off their insignia at school, making it more difficult for gangs to form and to set themselves apart from the other students.

Additionally, weapons and guns, which are often times hidden under loose fitting clothes, cannot be brought to school that easily anymore. Also, because everybody wears the same outfits, expensive designer clothing is no longer stolen at school. As former President Clinton said in his 1996 State of the Union Address, "If it means teenagers will stop killing each other over designer jackets, then public schools should be able to require school uniforms" (qtd. in Vital Speeches).

Many parents argue that adopting a school uniform policy into their children's public school would be too expensive, and therefore, not every parent could afford it. As LBUSD Board President Karin Polachek points out, though,

> Affordable school uniforms can reduce clothing costs substantially. The average clothing cost per child in schools with a student uniform is markedly less than that in schools without uniforms. The typical uniforms cost $65-75 per year for a set of three – far less than some students spend for one item of designer clothing. Basic uniforms may be obtained at local thrift stores, department stores or uniform suppliers. ("School Uniform")

Polacheck's statement is further supported by the fact that "[f]inancial assistance is available to disadvantaged children from indigent families. Privately funded – at no taxpayer expense – local organizations have provided more than $16,000 in uniforms to Long Beach children" ("School Uniform").

While opponents of the school uniform policy try to defend their standpoint that uniforms take away the student's individuality, they seem to overlook that individuality is expressed through much more than the clothes a person is wearing. If students, as well as parents, think that their outfits are a major part of their personality, they should consider that students would still be allowed to express themselves in their afternoon activities and on the weekends. Personally, if I would have to make the decision again between a pro-uniform policy and one that does not require school uniforms, I would probably vote for adopting uniforms into my public school because the benefits I now see in it outweigh the imagined loss of individuality.

Troeger 5

Works Cited

Clinton, William. "State of the Union 1996: The Age of Possibility." <u>Vital Speeches</u> 62 (1996): 258+. WebPals. Century College Lib., White Bear Lake, MN. 1 Mar. 2005 <http://www.pals.msus.edu>.

"Go Figure: Uniformity Rules." <u>Ladies Home Journal</u> Oct. 2000: 72.

Polacheck, Karin. "Long Beach Press-Telegram – Letter from Board President." <u>LBUSD Uniform Policy</u>. 17 Mar. 2005 <http://www.lbusd.k12.ca.us/uniform/uniformf.htm>.

"School Uniform Fact Sheet." <u>LBUSD Uniform Policy</u>. 17 Mar. 2005 <http://www.lbusd.k12.ca.us/uniform/uniforma.htm>.

Identifying Sources and Introducing Source Material

Quotations have two key purposes in essays about literature: to exemplify claims and to reproduce the language of the source. Effectively introducing quotations and paraphrased material is important for several reasons. First, you need to distinguish your ideas from the ideas of other writers. Quotation marks obviously are one way to make this distinction, but giving the author's/authority's name gives greater emphasis to the material. Also, when readers see quotation marks, they may wonder about the writer of the quoted passage. They will also more easily distinguish the different approaches of the various critics. Third, giving an author's name illustrates differences between your primary and secondary sources that might not otherwise be clear. Finally, it is a form of courtesy. Giving credit to the words and ideas of other people in your text is an acknowledgement of their help.

Identify quotations for primary sources by identifying the author, the work, and the context of the quotation:

At the climax of Hawthorne's "Young Goodman Brown," Brown's

inability to seek redemption and his loss of hope is signaled by his

cry of despair:

" 'My Faith is gone!' cried he after one stupefied moment. 'There is

no good on earth; and sin is but a name' " (238).

Identify quotations from secondary sources by giving the author's name:

Judith Fetterly suggests that "A Rose for Emily" is "an exposure of how this act [imposing feminine ideals on women] in turn defines and recoils upon men" (493).

Or, identify quotations from secondary sources by giving the author's claim to authority:

One prominent Faulkner critic claims that "the violence contained in the rotted corpse of Homer Barron is the mirror image of the violence represented in the tableau, the back-flung front door flung back with a vengeance" (Fetterly 493).

Documentation Guide for In-Text Citations

In most English classes, you will probably be required to use the MLA style of in-text citation (also referred to as parenthetical citation) recommended for papers in literature and the humanities. MLA style is widely used and accepted for papers written in other fields; however, your instructor may ask you to use APA style if you write on a subject in the social sciences. Instead of using numbered footnotes, writers who follow the MLA style refer to sources by making abbreviated in-text references within parentheses. These citations refer to the sources listed on the Works Cited section at the end of the paper.

Let's assume, for example, that you're quoting from a novel. The sentence in which the quote is used might read as follows:

The atheist that Zane encounters here believes that "oblivion is the greatest gift."

You let the reader know where this quote comes from by using a parenthetical reference as follows:

The atheist that Zane encounters here believes that "oblivion is the greatest gift" (Anthony 147).

The information in parentheses refers the reader to the following entry on the Works Cited list:

Anthony, Piers. <u>On a Pale Horse</u>. New York: Ballantine, 1983.

The form of this abbreviated reference depends upon the amount of information you include in your introduction to the material. Here are some guidelines for the most common situations.

Author mentioned in the text
If you include the author's name as you introduce the material, put only the page number(s) within parentheses:

Baldwin says his father "never forgave the white world for

having saddled him with a Christ in whom [...] they

themselves no longer believed" (139).

Author not mentioned in the text
If you introduce material without mentioning the author's name, use only the author's last name followed by the page number(s) within parentheses:

The author says his father "never forgave the white world

for having saddled him with a Christ in whom [...] they

themselves no longer believed" (Baldwin 139).

Citing more than one work by the same author or a work without an author
If you have more than one work by the same author on your Works Cited list, you must use an abbreviated title in your parenthetical reference so that your readers know to which

work you are referring. If you use the author's name in the sentence, you only need the title and page number(s) in the parenthetical reference. If you do not use the author's name in the sentence, the parenthetical reference should contain the author's last name followed by a comma, the title of the work you are citing, and the page number. (If the work has no discernible author, use an abbreviated title followed by the page number.)

Orwell repeatedly assailed the use of clichés and stale

metaphors because "they have lost all evocative power and

are merely used because they save people the trouble of

inventing phrases for themselves" (Politics 145). The term

"duckspeak" is used to describe this practice because the

harsh gabble of inner party members sounded "almost like

the quacking of a duck" (Orwell, Nineteen 23).

ᴧ   **Long quotations**
Quotations of more than four typed lines must be set off from the text. Indent the quote one inch (ten spaces) from the left margin, double space, and place the citation after the final period. Quotations that are indented do not need to have quotation marks put around them:

As Singer indicates, events in the seventeenth century

foreshadow the Holocaust:

Sixteen years before, the Cossack hetman, Bogdan

Chmiel-micki, had led an army of haidamak troops in

insurrection against the Polish landowners; enroute,

they had fallen upon another target of their wrath, the

Jewish townsfolk, the lord's stewards. It has been

estimated that 100,000 Jews perished during the

years from 1648-1658. (8)

⋏ **A work with more than one author**

If you refer to a work with two or three authors without
mentioning their names in the text, give all their last names in
the citation:

In some of the Greek creation myths, Time was first in

order of creation: "The legendary poet Orpheus is said [...]

to have believed that TIME came first, existing from the

very beginning, but without a beginning" (Robinson and

Wilson 79).

If you are citing a source with more than three authors, use et
al., which means "and the others," after the name of one of the
authors:

A nurse has to use a variety of sources in making a

diagnosis: "The sources are many: the patient, his chart,

the Kardex, the patient's relatives or visitors, hospital

personal, and the nurse's own knowledge" (Matheney et al.

27).

⋏ **Corporate author**

When referring to a corporate author, use the name of the
organization or institution if you haven't mentioned it in the
text. Use common abbreviations to shorten names where
possible:

One significant source of heat loss is the "chimney effect":

"When air in a building is warmer than the outside air, the

entire building acts like a chimney—hot air tends to rise

and leak out of cracks at the upper levels and sucks cold

air in through cracks at the lower levels" (NSP 24-25).

⅄ **A work in more than one volume**
When citing a work in two or more volumes, use a colon
between the volume number and page number:

Being "disgusted" with the way the entrepreneurs

"oppressed and neglected" the proletariat, [Orwell] became

a pro-socialist ("Collected Essays" 3: 403).

⅄ **A poem**
To refer to lines from a poem, parenthetical citations should
contain only the line number(s):

The speaker in "The Man He Killed" hesitates when

explaining why he killed a man in battle: "I shot him dead

because – / Because he was my foe" (9-10).

Note the conventional practice of placing a slash (/) to show
the end of each line (line 9 in this case) for short poetry
quotations not set off from the text by the indenting of the left
margin.

⅄ **An electronic source with no page numbers**
If you are citing an internet source without screen or
paragraph numbers, include the author's name in an
introductory phrase in your text or in a parenthetical citation.
If the author's name is unavailable but you are certain the

source is reliable and have decided to use it, include the article title, shortened if possible, enclosed in quotation marks in a parenthetical citation.

a. Internet source with an author, but no page, screen, or paragraph numbers.

   "A Western U.S. drought that began eight years ago has continued after the reprieve of a couple of wet years" (White).

b. Internet source without an author or page, screen, or paragraph numbers.

   "Population growth, especially in rapidly growing parts of greater Clark County (NV) and Maricopa County (AZ) is only partly to blame for the coming water shortage" ("Global Warming Brings Water Shortage").

Be sure to begin the Works Cited entry for each of these sources with the information that appears in your in-text or parenthetical citation.

ᴧ   The Bible
Cite passages in the Bible by placing the abbreviated book title and the chapter and verse numbers within parentheses directly after the passage:

   Job complains of the cruelty of his friends: "How long do

   you afflict my soul, and break me in pieces with words?

   Behold, these ten times you confound me, and are not

   ashamed to oppress me" (Job 19.2-3).

ᴧ   An interview
Carefully introduce an interview with the name of the person interviewed; otherwise, no other in-text citation is necessary. If you do not use the name of the person interviewed in the sentence, cite the work like any other by placing the

interviewed person's name in parenthesis at the end of the sentence. The interview will appear later on the Works Cited page under the person's last name.

Preparing the Works Cited Page

At the end of your research paper, place a list of the sources you have used in your paper. This is your "Works Cited" list.

A Few Basic Set-up Guidelines:

Alphabetize the sources by the last name of the author(s). If the author of one of your sources is unknown, begin the entry with the title, and alphabetize by the first word in the title (other than "A," "An," or "The").

Double-space the Works Cited page.

Underline the titles of longer works, such as novels, book-length essays, and plays. Journal and magazine titles are also underlined. *Note: Even though MLA format currently uses underlining for longer works, some instructors prefer italics, so pay attention to your instructor's requirements. Remain consistent.*

Place the titles of shorter works, such as short stories, essays, or periodical articles, in quotation marks. If you are citing a short work that is part of a longer work, such as a story published in an anthology or an essay in a book, place the title of the shorter work in quotations, and underline the title of the longer work.

Consult the <u>MLA Handbook</u>. The following examples illustrate the MLA form for some common types of sources. If you have a source that is not listed here, consult the <u>MLA Handbook</u> (which can be found in the Writing Center or the library) or the websites listed on the "Resources" page of Chapter Two. (The explanation format below has been borrowed from <u>Documenting Sources Across the Curriculum</u>, companion booklet to the eighth edition of the <u>Little, Brown Handbook</u>.)

Punctuate precisely. Punctuation is very important in the Works Cited page. Be sure to follow all models *EXACTLY* as they appear, including putting in periods and commas and using one space (and only one space) after each punctuation mark.

Shorten the name of the publisher (often to a single word): "Little" for Little, Brown; "Knopf" for Alfred A. Knopf. For university presses, use the abbreviations "U" and "P" (i.e., Oxford UP). If the title page lists an imprint and a publisher—for instance, Vintage Books and Random House—give both names with a hyphen: "Vintage-Random."

Capitalize important words even if the original source does not. The first letters of the first and last words in each title must be capitalized. In addition, the first letters of all important words also need to be capitalized. Articles (a, an, the), prepositions (between, in, on, to), and coordinating conjunctions (and, but, so) do not need to be capitalized. For a complete list of articles, prepositions, and coordinating conjunctions, visit the Writing Center.

Listing Books

The basic format for a book includes the following elements:

1. *Author's Name.* Give the full last name followed by a comma, the full first name, and any initial. Leave out titles, including Dr., PhD, etc.

2. *Title.* Give the full title, including any subtitle. Underline books, etc., and put essay titles in quotation marks. Capitalize the first letters of the first and last words and other important words.

Anderson, Paul. The Merman's Children. New York: Berkley, 1979.

3. *City of Publication.* Use the first city listed on the title page. Do not include states unless directed by your instructor.

4. *Publisher.* Give the name of the publisher. Leave out words such as "Books," "Inc.," and "Company," etc. (examples on next page).

5. *Copyright Year.* Give the most recent copyright year only.

A book with one author

Anderson, Paul. <u>The Merman's Children</u>. New York: Berkley,

    1979.

Two or more books by the same author

James, Henry. <u>The Ambassadors</u>. Richfield: Pearson, 1964.

---. <u>The Golden Bowl</u>. New York: Dell, 1974.

A book with two or three authors

Brandy, Leo, and Morris Dickstein. <u>Great Film Directors</u>.

    London: Oxford UP, 1964.

A book with more than three authors

Sheehan, Neil, et al. <u>The Pentagon Papers</u>. Baltimore:

    Bantam, 1971.

A book by a corporate author

Boston Women's Health Book Collective. <u>Our Bodies,</u>

    <u>Ourselves</u>. 2nd ed. New York: Simon, 1978.

A book by an anonymous author

<u>Sir Gawain and the Green Knight</u>. Grand Rapids: Bantam,

    1984.

A book with an editor

Percy, Charles, ed. <u>The Cambridge Book of Literary</u>

    <u>Anecdotes</u>. London: Cambridge UP, 1992.

ᴧ **A book with an author and an editor**

George, E.. <u>Foxes</u>. Ed. Myra Gold. Chicago: Fleetwood,

1942.

ᴧ **An anthology or a compilation**

Edel, Leon, and Percy Lubbock, eds. <u>Henry James: Essays</u>

<u>in Criticism</u>. Detroit: Knopf, 1964.

ᴧ **A work in an anthology**

Jackson, Shirley. "The Lottery." <u>The Story and Its Writer</u>.

Ed. Ann Charters. New York: St. Martin's, 1983.

942-49.

ᴧ **An introduction, a preface, a foreword, or an afterward**

Marcus, Steven. Afterward. <u>Nicholas Nickleby</u>. By Charles

Dickens. Boston: New American Library, 1982. 812-

39.

ᴧ **A book with more than one volume**

Cowie, Peter. <u>A Concise History of the Cinema</u>. Vol. 2. New

York: Barnes, 1971. 2 vols.

ᴧ **An edition other than the first**

Century College English Department. <u>Century College</u>

<u>English Handbook</u>. 3rd ed. Richfield: Pearson, 2002.

ᴧ   **A book in a series** (Use series number after series name.)

McClave, Heather, ed. <u>Women Writers of the Short Story</u>.

Twentieth Century Views 7. Englewood Cliffs:

Prentice, 1980.

ᴧ   **A word or definition taken from a dictionary**

"Baleful." <u>Merriam-Webster's Collegiate Dictionary.</u> 11th

ed. 2005.

ᴧ   **A signed article in a reference book**

Jones, John. "Arizona." <u>Encyclopedia Britannica</u>. 1993 ed.

ᴧ   **An unsigned article in a reference book**

"The Punic and Macedonian Wars." <u>An Encyclopedia of</u>

<u>World History</u>. Ed. William L. Langer. 52nd ed.

Boston: Houghton, 1952. 85-91.

"Arizona." <u>Encyclopedia Britannica</u>. 1993 ed.

ᴧ   **A reprinted article in a reference book**

Gorman, Thomas R. "Faulkner's Ethical Point of View." <u>CEA</u>

<u>Critic</u> 28.8 (1966): 4-6. Rpt. in <u>Short Story Criticism</u>.

Ed. Laurie L. Harris and Sheila Fitzgerald. Vol. 1.

Detroit: Gale, 1988. 165-67.

Flint, I. L.. <u>Spies I've Loved</u>. n.p.: Twayne, 1967. Rpt. in

<u>Short Story Criticism</u>. Ed. Laurie L. Harris and

Sheila Fitzgerald. Vol. 12. Detroit: Gale, 1989. 233-47.

▲ **A government publication**

United States. Cong. House Committee on the Judiciary. Immigration and Nationality Act with Amendments and Notes on Related Laws. 101st Cong., 1st sess. 23 vols. Washington: GPO, 1980.

▲ **Published proceedings of a conference**

Griggs, John, ed. AIDS: Public Policy Dimensions. Proc. of International AIDS Awareness Conf., Jan. 1986, New York U. New York: United Hospital Fund, 1987.

▲ **A translation**

Boulle, Pierre. Planet of the Apes. Trans. Xan Fielding. New York: Signet, 1963.

▲ **A book with a title in its title**

Robbins, John. Perspectives on Huckleberry Finn: Nature and Community. New York: Oxford UP, 1985.

▲ **An unpublished dissertation**

Nesset, Michael. "John Updike and Andrew Wyeth: The Nostalgic Mode in Contemporary American

Art." Diss. U of Minnesota, 1978.

A published dissertation

DeMuth, James. <u>Finley Peter Dunne</u>. Diss. U of Minnesota,

1976. Carbondale: Southern Illinois UP, 1979.

Listing Periodicals: Magazines, Newspapers, and Journals

The basic format for an article from a magazine or newspaper includes the following information:

1. *Author's Name.* Give full last name followed by a comma, the full first name, and any initial. Leave out titles, including Dr., PhD, etc.

2. *Article Title.* Give the full article title in quotation marks. Capitalize the first letters of the first and last words and other important words.

3. *Periodical/Newspaper Title.* Give the full title, including any subtitle. Capitalize the first letters of the first and last words and other important words. Omit articles.

4. *Date.* Give the date of publication. Give the day first, then the abbreviated month, followed by the year.

5. *Page Numbers.* The inclusive page numbers of the article (without the abbreviation "pp."). See "Tips" for more details.

Roth, Philip. "My Baseball Years." <u>New York Times</u> 2 Apr. 1973: 35.

The basic format for an article from a scholarly journal includes the following information:

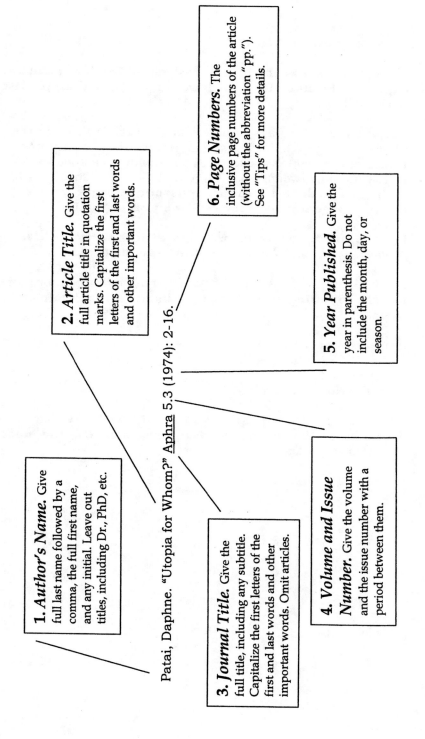

2. *Article Title.* Give the full article title in quotation marks. Capitalize the first letters of the first and last words and other important words.

6. *Page Numbers.* The inclusive page numbers of the article (without the abbreviation "pp."). See "Tips" for more details.

5. *Year Published.* Give the year in parenthesis. Do not include the month, day, or season.

Patai, Daphne. "Utopia for Whom?" <u>Aphra</u> 5.3 (1974): 2-16.

1. *Author's Name.* Give full last name followed by a comma, the full first name, and any initial. Leave out titles, including Dr., PhD, etc.

3. *Journal Title.* Give the full title, including any subtitle. Capitalize the first letters of the first and last words and other important words. Omit articles.

4. *Volume and Issue Number.* Give the volume and the issue number with a period between them.

Tips for Avoiding Mistakes:

Make sure you **use the format designated for your publication type**. (i.e., Be sure that if you have found a periodical, you use the periodical format.)

Use the inclusive page numbers of the article (without the abbreviation "pp."). For the second number in inclusive page numbers over 100, provide only as many digits as needed for clarity (usually two): 87-88, 100-01, 398-401, 1026-36, 1190-206. **If the article does not run on consecutive pages, provide only the first page number followed by a plus sign: 16+.**

If you don't have an author, begin with the article title. Alphabetize in the Works Cited page accordingly.

According to the MLA Handbook, if you are missing information, **use the following abbreviations** to indicate what information is missing:

n.p. = No Place.
n.p. = No Publisher.
n.d. = No Date.
n. pag. = No Page Numbers.

The volume, date, and page number format will vary slightly depending on the kind of periodical being cited. **Use the models on the following pages**.

A signed article from a daily newspaper (The page number should be listed as it appears in the paper.)

Roth, Philip. "My Baseball Years." <u>New York Times</u> 2 Apr.

1973: 35.

An unsigned article from a daily newspaper (The page number should be listed as it appears in the paper.)

"Temperature Hits Record Low." <u>St. Paul Pioneer Press</u> 12

Jan. 1988: 11A.

An article from a monthly or bimonthly magazine

Wills, Garry. "The Words That Remade America: Lincoln at

Gettysburg." <u>Atlantic</u> June 1992: 57-79.

Byers, Sandra. "Gettysburg Revisited." <u>Politics Today</u> Mar.-

Apr. 2002: 77-9.

An article from a weekly or biweekly magazine

Scholl, Jage. "Mutual Funds: The End of an Era." <u>Barron's</u>

19 May 1986: 44.

An article in a journal with continuous pagination
This type of scholarly journal begins each issue continuing from the page number of the previous issue. Its citation looks different than a journal with separate pagination in that it does not include an issue number.

Stewart, D.H. "Vanity Fair: Life in the Void." <u>College English</u>

25 (1963): 209-14.

no period

⋏ **An article in a journal with separate pagination for each issue**

Patai, Daphne. "Utopia for Whom?" <u>Aphra</u> 5.3 (1974): 2-16.

⋏ **An editorial**

"Minimum Wage." Editorial. <u>Star-Tribune</u> [Minneapolis] 11

July 1996: A22.

⋏ **A book review**

Robbins, George. "Whither Fiction?" Rev. of <u>Out of Work</u>, by

Greg Mulcahy. <u>Star-Tribune</u> [Minneapolis] 11 Mar.

1994: 12E.

⋏ **An abstract from Dissertation Abstracts International**

Dojka-Loupe, Stefanie. "Patterns of Desire: The Novels of

Jane Austen." Diss. U of Minnesota, 1982. DAI 43

(1982): 2799A.

Listing Electronic Sources

Electronic sources include those available on CD-ROM and those available online, such as an Internet document or a database accessed online. Similar to citations of print sources, citations of online sources require available information such as author, title, and date of publication (date of online posting or last revision for an online source), but online sources also require two special pieces of information:

1. **Give the date when you consulted the source as well as the date (if available) when the source was posted or updated online.** The posting date comes first, with the

other publication information. Your access date falls near the end of the entry, just before the electronic address.

2. **Give the source's exact electronic address enclosed in angle brackets (<>).** Usually you'll find the address in your Web browser's "Location" or "Address" field near the top of the screen as you're viewing the source. (Be sure to give the complete address for the specific page you are using, not just for the site's home page.) Place the address at the end of the entry. If you must break an address from one line to the next, do so only after a slash, and do not hyphenate.

Because of the great variety of types of sources that can be accessed online, it is important to identify what kind of source you're looking at. Just because the information is on a screen doesn't mean it can be cited in the same manner as a similar looking source.

Additionally, although most of these examples show an author for the material, it is not uncommon for electronic sources to be anonymous or authored by a corporate author. If the source is anonymous, begin your citation with the title instead of the author's name, and alphabetize accordingly. If the source is written by a corporate author, list the corporation or organization as the author. It should be mentioned that sources that are anonymous or from obscure providers will be seen by your instructors and your readers as less reliable sources.

The following models illustrate methods for documenting some common source types but are by no means definitive. Consult with your instructors about their preferences for electronic citations, and make use of resource books in the Century College Writing Center or Library if you are unsure which format to use. Be sure to consult other handbooks and Internet sites for the most current methods of documentation.

The basic format for a website (note that this is one, multiple line entry):

1. *Author's Name.* Give full last name followed by a comma, the full first name, and any initial. Leave out titles, including Dr., PhD, etc.

2. *Article or Document Title.* Give the full article or document title in quotation marks. Capitalize the first letters of the first and last words and other important words.

Smith, John. "Passengers Rescued from Sinking Cruise Ship off Alaska." CNN.com. 14 May 2007.

3. *Website Title.* Give the full title, including any subtitle. Capitalize the first letters of the first and last words and other important words. This is usually the homepage for your document.

4. *Copyright or Last Updated Date.* Give the date of publication. Give the day first, then the abbreviated month, followed by the year.

Cable News Network. 12 June 2007

<http://www.cnn.com/2007/US/05/14/alaska.ship/index.html>.

5. *Sponsor.* Give the sponsoring organization (if any is listed).

6. *Access Date.* Give the date you accessed the site.

7. *Web Address.* Give the full web address enclosed in < > brackets.

Tips for Avoiding Mistakes:

Make sure you **use the format designated for your publication type**. (i.e., Be sure that if you have used a library subscription service, you use the designated format.)

Use page numbers only if you have a PDF file of the actual document. When you print a document from the Internet, the printer will automatically list the pages, usually designating them "1 of 2" and so forth. THESE ARE NOT THE PAGE NUMBERS FOR YOUR PUBLICATION. Do not use these numbers in your Works Cited page or in your in-text citations unless directed by your instructor.

If you don't have an author, begin with the article/document title. Alphabetize in the Works Cited page accordingly.

Google, Yahoo, and Ask.com are search engines, not homepages. To find your document's homepage, delete everything in the web address following the .com, .org, .gov, etc., extensions. This should take you to the homepage for your document.

According to the MLA Handbook, if you are missing information, **use the following abbreviations** to indicate what information is missing:

n.d. = No Date.
n. pag. = No page numbers. (Use only if you are citing an online
          periodical article, not if you are citing a regular website.)

The formats will vary slightly depending on the kind of periodical being cited. **Use the models on the following pages**.

▲ **A CD-ROM**

Clute, John, and Peter Nicholls. "Time Paradoxes." The

Multimedia Encyclopedia of Science Fiction. CD-

ROM. Danbury: Grolier, 1995.

Dickens, Charles. "England Under Edward the First, called

Longshanks." A Child's History of England. Ed. John

Smith. Oxford: Oxford UP, 1922. 20-43. History of

the World. CD-ROM. Parsippany: Bureau of

Electronic Publishing, 1994.

▲ **A document from a scholarly project or an information database**

McNally, Amy. "Hisaye Yamamoto." Voices From the Gaps:

Women Writers of Color. Ed. Kim Surkan, et al. U of

Minnesota P, 1999. U of Minnesota Women's

Studies. 9 Jan. 2002 <http://voices.cla.umn.edu/

authors/HisayeYamamoto.html>.

▲ **An article accessed through a subscription service, such as WebPals, EBSCO, MnLink, Electric Library, or Infotrac**

If you have the following EBSCO information:

Database:	Academic Search Premier
Citation:	The Explicator Spring 1998, v56, n3, p129(2)
Author:	Gruesser, John

Title: Poe's "The Cask of Amontillado." by
John Gruesser

Your citation will look like this:

Gruesser, John. "Poe's 'The Cask of Amontillado.'" The

Explicator 56.3 (1998): 129-30. Academic Search

Premier. EBSCO. Century College Lib.,White Bear

Lake, MN. 6 June 2007

<http://web.ebscohost.com>.

If you have the following Infotrac information:

Title: Poe's 'The Cask of Amontillado'
Database: Expanded Academic ASAP
Authors: Cervo, Nathan
From: The Explicator, Spring 1993, v51, n3,
                 p155(2)

Your citation will look like this:

Cervo, Nathan. "Poe's 'The Cask of Amontillado.'" The

Explicator 51.3 (1993): 155-56. Expanded Academic

ASAP. Gale. Century College Lib., White Bear Lake,

MN. 8 Jan. 2006 <http://infotrac.galegroup.com>.

A document from a professional website

Womack, Martha. "The Cask of Amontillado." Poedecoder.

12 Apr. 2001. 3 Jan. 2002

<http://www.poedecoder.com>.

⅄ **A document from a personal homepage**

Davis, Marie. Home Page. 17 Mar. 2005. 3 May 2005

      <http://mariedavis.hackish.net>.

⅄ **An article in an online magazine or newspaper**

Cave, Damien. "File Sharing: Innocent Until Proven Guilty."

      Salon 13 June 2002. Salon Media Group. 14 June

      2002 <http://www.salon.com/tech/feature/

      2002/06/13/liebowitz/index.html>.

An unsigned article on an online news site

"Passengers Rescued from Sinking Cruise Ship off Alaska."

      CNN.com. 14 May 2007. Cable News Network. 12

      June 2007 <http://www.cnn.com/2007/US/05/

      14/alaska.ship/index.html>.

⅄ **An unsigned article in an online encyclopedia or reference work**

"Hungary." The Encyclopedia of World History: Ancient

      Medieval and Modern. Ed. Peter N. Stearns. 6th ed.

      Boston: Houghton, 2001. 14 June 2002

      <http://www.bartleby.com/67/1245.html>.

Listing Other Sources

⋏ **A film**

The Pink Panther. Dir. Blake Edwards. Perf. Peter Sellers,

David Niven, Robert Wagner, Claudia Cardinale.

MGM, 1963.

A radio or television program

Biederman and the Firebugs. Writ. Max Frisch. Prod.

Bayrischer Rundfunk. BBC International, Munich.

13 Mar. 1953.

"The Hero's Adventure." Moyers: Joseph Campbell and the

Power of Myth. Prod. Catherine Tatge. PBS. WNET,

New York. 23 May 1988.

⋏ **A performance**

An Inspector Calls. By J.B. Priestly. Dir. Stephen Daldry.

Perf. Stacy Keach and Kenneth Cranham. Ordway

Music Theater, St. Paul. 11 July 1996.

⋏ **A sound recording**

Beethoven, Ludwig. The Complete Symphonies. City of

Birmingham Symphony Orch. Cond. Walter Weller.

MHS, 1994.

The Beatles. "A Day in the Life." By John Lennon and Paul

McCartney. <u>Sgt. Pepper's Lonely Hearts Club Band</u>.

LP. EMI, 1967.

⅄ **A work of art**

da Vinci, Leonardo. <u>La Gioconda</u>. Louvre, Paris.

Rodin, Auguste. <u>The Thinker</u>. Rodin Museum, Paris.

⅄ **A map or chart**

<u>Hennepin County</u>. Map. St. Paul: MN Dept. of

Transportation, 1994.

⅄ **A cartoon**

Sack, Steve. Cartoon. <u>Star-Tribune</u> [Minneapolis] 10 July

1996: 22A.

⅄ **An advertisement**

Meade Instruments Corp. Advertisement. <u>Sky and Telescope</u>

Nov. 1994: 117.

⅄ **A published or an unpublished letter**

O'Connor, Flannery. "To Sally Fitzgerald." 1 July 1962. <u>The</u>

<u>Habit of Being</u>. Ed. Sally Fitzgerald. New York:

Scribner's, 1968. 210-11.

Brown, John. Letter to his wife. 3 Nov. 1858. Manuscript

collection. Washington U Library, St. Louis.

ᴧ **An interview conducted by the researcher**

Sexton, Ann. Personal interview. 25 July 1970.

ᴧ **A lecture, a speech or an address**

Turner, Paige. "Death by Documentation." Millenium

College, Falcon Crest, AR. 14 Aug. 2007.

Clinton, William. "Inaugural Address." The Capitol,

Washington, DC. 20 Jan. 1993.

Chapter Four:
Writing About Literature

Like physics, mathematics, sociology, and history, literature gives us information about the world in which we live. However, unlike the sciences and social sciences, literature is able to present the world from irrational and/or highly emotional points of view, as in the stream-of-consciousness narratives of William Faulkner and Virginia Woolf. Literary works report on the full range of human experience; thus, they extend and enrich our knowledge of the world and are an important part of a college education.

As well as being a composition course, English 1022 introduces you to the study of literature. The goal of your 1022 instructor will be to teach you critical reading of texts. This means that you will spend time focusing on the interpretation and analysis of literary works. If you master these skills, you will be able to write well about any of the poems, stories, plays, novels, or other texts assigned in English 1022.

How to Write About Literature

Your instructor will require you to observe several rules in the essays that you write about literature.

▲   *Authors' names*: The first time you mention an author's name in your essay, use the first, middle (if used in your source), and last name. *After that, use the last name only. It is never correct to refer to an author by his or her first name only.*

▲   *Literary present*: It is customary to refer to events in a story, novel, or poem in the present tense even though the events took place long ago. Thus Odysseus *slaughters* the suitors, Huck Finn *journeys* down the Mississippi, the Bible salesman *seduces* Hulga Hopewell and *steals* her wooden leg, and so on. For exceptions to the present-tense rule, consult your instructor.

⅄ *Genre or type of literature*: Be specific about the type of literature you are discussing in your essay. <u>Huckleberry Finn</u> is a novel, not a book. <u>Walden</u> and "A Hanging" are essays, not stories.

Writing About Fiction and Poetry

Some of your essays in English 1022 may be about fiction stories or about poetry. You may be required to examine the use of language, imagery, and/or symbolism in a particular poem or you may discuss poetic devices such as stanza form, repetition, grammatical pauses, or dialogue. You may also discuss the historical or biographical background of a poem. In writing about fiction, you may consider such topics as plot structure, point of view, characterization, and style. Because the fiction writer employs many of the same techniques of the poet, you may also analyze imagery, symbolism, allegory, irony, and satire within particular stories.

For both poetry and fiction analyses, you may write short papers focusing on limited passages or aspects of the work. You may also be asked to write longer papers that present a more complete analysis of a poem or story. Sometimes you will be asked to write an interpretation, and occasionally you will be asked to write a comparison/contrast paper about two poems, two characters, two stories, etc.

A Sample Poetry Analysis Essay

The following paper is an example of a typical poetry analysis paper for a 1022 class. Note how the writer has incorporated words or passages, directly quoting them from the poem, in order to develop her analysis.

Jane Doe   Doe 1

Dr. Smith

English 1022.01

2 Mar. 2007

<h3 style="text-align:center">Do Not Fear Death</h3>

Many people can't help having a fear of death. It seems to be a huge force that comes, and we are powerless to stop it. Wislawa Szymborska's poem "On Death, Without Exaggeration" takes a different stand. The speaker in this poem seems to belittle death and points out its failures. The poem tells the reader that there should be no fear of death for it can not take away what was life.

Symborska does a great job of making the reader feel superior to death. By capitalizing the word "death," she gives the reader the impression of death being a person. The fact that death, like us, can fail also helps to give it a human likeness. If a person sees death as human, then he or she may be less intimidated by it. The poem points out that death can only kill; it cannot take part in the events that are associated with its aftermath. Some examples given of actions that death cannot do are "dig a grave/ [or] make a coffin" (10-11), which are both activities that are left for people to take care of after death. One may be the idea that death is lazy and unable to finish its own work. These kinds of feelings may make someone reading the poem look down at death instead of cowering in fear of it.

When describing the way death goes about taking life, the speaker says, "Preoccupied with killing, / it does the job awkwardly, / As though each of us were its first kill" (13-15). These lines seem to show the audience that death is clumsy. Death has been killing since life began yet still lacks the skill to plan out these killings. Instead, death is hasty and awkward. The speaker also points out that although death does have its accomplishments, it has many failures as well.

The poem tells readers to look at death's "missed blow, / and repeat attempts" (19-20). Death doesn't always complete its work and often fails when trying. This suggests that people have outsmarted death. They have dodged death's blows, and it has had to come and make its attempt again. It almost seems as if the speaker is showing the audience how people are winning against death.

In the next stanza, the speaker tries to tell the audience that death is weak by saying, "Sometimes it isn't strong enough/ to swat a fly from the air" (21-22). Since flies are sometimes seen as weaker than human beings, if death can't beat a fly, then why should people fear it?

Closer to the end of Szymborska's poem, the speaker begins to tell readers what death's ultimate failure is. Lines 33-34 state, "Hearts still beat inside eggs/ Babies' skeletons grow." This quote illustrates that even with death taking life, life is still being made. One may get the sense that death can't keep up with humans. For every life death takes, there is still more life being born. While many readers can't help feeling that death is a powerful force over them, the speaker claims that those who think this are "living proof/ that [death] is not" (38-39). The speaker means that those who are alive prove alone that death is not so powerful.

The speaker calls humans immortal by saying:

> There's no life
> that couldn't be immortal
> if only for a moment.
>
> Death
> always arrives by that very moment too late. (40-44)

Perhaps immortality is not living forever but having lived at all. It can be experienced in a moment, and the fact that people have existed at all, in a way, makes them immortal. The last lines in this poem put it all together: "As far as you've come/ can't be undone" (47-48). Even after one has died, Death still can't take away what was his or her life.

This poem is important because it illustrates that life is bigger than death. It may make people appreciate life more because life is what remains once death has come. Szymborska shows why readers should not be afraid of death in a way that can truly convince. Even if death ends a life, it can't take back what's already been done. That, after all, is what death tries to accomplish. In some ways, human beings have outdone death, and it really has no power over humanity. In the end, people have lived, and in that sense, they have won.

Doe 4

Work Cited

Szymborska, Wislawa. "On Death, Without Exaggeration." Trans.
Stanislaw Baranczak and Clare Cavanaugh. <u>Making Literature
Matter: An Anthology for Readers and Writers</u>. Ed. John Schilb
and John Clifford. Boston: Bedford, 2000. 1535-36.

A Sample 1022 Documented Essay

When researching a literary topic and using information for a documented essay, you will want to follow the methods explained in Chapter Three on how to cite sources. Nevertheless, there are some specifics to follow when citing literary sources. (See the previous poetry paper for help on how to quote lines of poetry). Most often, the literary research paper will require you to consider others' interpretations of the literary work you have read. You should use the critique of others to formulate your *own* interpretation of the piece. In a longer analysis, you should *not* simply summarize another's point of view.

The following essay is a variation on a strictly literary topic. Although the essay does not cover a particular individual work, the writer focuses on a well-defined topic and presents a clear perspective on that topic, incorporating several sources within the discussion.

Sal Smith   Smith 1

Dr. Story

English 1022.01

7 May 2007

More than Movies

The James Bond movies have inspired a wealth of popular culture that both feeds on and rivals the success of the movies themselves. Bond movie posters have ably fulfilled their marketing aims over the decades and are now considered collectable art. Any new addition to the Bond canon includes in its pre-release hype the fact that the theme song is performed by a current or recent chart-topping singer. Even before the theme song announcement, there is the question that makes many viewers salivate in anticipation: Who will play the next Bond Girl? For a cadre of actresses, from Ursula Andress in 1962's <u>Dr. No</u> to Halle Berry in 2002's <u>Die Another Day</u>, their roles as Bond Girls have distinguished their careers for many audience members. More than just movies, the James Bond franchise has contributed to the world art, music, and feminine ideals.

The poster art of James Bond films has added to the popular imagery of the franchise, serving both to market individual movies and to increase the mystique of the entire series. The primary features of the posters have for decades reinforced the popular expectations for the movies: fight scenes, vehicle chases, and women in skimpy, exotic costumes. Beyond this, the posters have also introduced images that became associated with the franchise even though they do not appear directly in the movies, such as the 007 icon joined with the silhouette of a Beretta, or Bond's stereotypical pose holding a gun across his chest (Nourmand 9). These artful advertisements are popular across a wide spectrum of collectors, and James Bond movie posters have sold at auction for as much as lithographs by more critically acclaimed artists such as Toulouse Lautrec (Nourmand 8-9). Thus, the popularity of the film franchise has carried over into the art world.

In the music world, the unique and memorable Bond film theme songs have served as prestige-building projects for singers, unknown and established alike. Dame Shirley Bassey started her United States career with the hit "Goldfinger" in 1964, and then went on to record "Diamonds Are Forever" (1972) and "Moonraker" (1979). She is the record-holder for the most Bond theme songs and has had continued recent success with History Repeating in 1997 and Diamonds are Forever – The Remix Album in 2000 ("Shirley Bassey"). In 1995, Tina Turner used her distinctive voice and style in the theme to Goldeneye, thereby increasing coverage of the release of Wildest Dreams, her first album since 1989. For the recent Bond entry, 2002's Die Another Day, the title song was performed by Madonna, a twenty-year veteran of stardom and certainly not suffering from underexposure. Her name is linked twice to the franchise since she also appeared in a minor role in the film. Quite clearly, prominent figures in the music business are not immune to the charms of 007 and his ongoing adventures.

In a similar vein, portraying a Bond Girl in just one film can be a career-defining role, following an actress for the rest of her life. Although most of the actresses continued to work in film post-Bond, and Berry won an Oscar for work done pre-Bond, it is their performances as Honey Rider, Kara Milovy and Jinx Johnson (to name a few) that are best-remembered by the movie-going public.

Smith 3

In 1999, renowned photographer Annie Leibovitz put together a spread for <u>Vanity Fair</u> magazine of a group of eighteen women, united by their participation in James Bond films over the series' 37-year span (D'Abo and Cork 7). One of these actresses is Maryam d'Abo, who plays Kara Milovy in <u>The Living Daylights</u> (1987). D'Abo was so intrigued by this chance to compare notes with fellow Bond Girls that she produced a documentary called <u>Bond Girls are Forever,</u> followed by a book of the same title in 2003. Both feature interviews with many actresses about their opinions of their characters, their experiences working on the films, and their views of how women are portrayed in cinema in general. D'Abo declares, "This book is a tribute to one of the lasting icons of feminine strength, beauty and resilience of the past half-century—the James Bond woman" (11).

Of the early films, Dana Broccoli, wife of longtime Bond producer Albert R. "Cubby" Broccoli, notes that "Bond women were nothing like the women in earlier films . . . I think that the female audiences were welcoming the change as were the men" (D'Abo and Cork 27). One aspect of that change was the forefront of the sexual revolution. To a generation of young women, writes Susan J. Douglas, "Sean Connery and a luscious Ursula Andress made it clear that unmarried men and women did have sex simply because they were attracted to each other . . . " (72). Furthermore, <u>Dr. No</u> set a tone for all subsequent Bond movies in the introduction of Andress' Honey Ryder—confidently, unselfconsciously arising from the sea in a white bikini, defiantly prepared to defend herself with her knife.

This change in the presentation of womanly ideals has continued into the 21st century. As Halle Berry said of her character,

Jinx Johnson (who makes her entrance to the Bond world wearing an orange bikini and a knife on her belt):

> ... she's the next step in the evolution of the Bond woman. Year after year they've gotten a little stronger, a little smarter, and more equally yoked with Bond. ... Jinx is really sexy ... as quick as Bond with the comeback lines and as tough as nails. That's the most empowered woman to me— someone who can be sexy and tough at the same time. (Collier 59)

Indeed, the impressions left by these women are so powerful that whatever else an actress may do in her career, she will always be a Bond Girl.

Over the past 40 years, the James Bond films have created for themselves particular associations in the public's awareness. Through poster art, music, and the everlasting allure of the Bond Girls, the 007 movie franchise has taken on a life outside of the megaplex and video store. Art professors and casual collectors spend time and money pursuing Bond movie posters. Bond movie theme songs have made at least one career and currently are embraced by already-successful singers. Actresses who portrayed Bond Girls decades ago are still photographed and interviewed in relation to their two hours of Bond fame. These incarnations of the James Bond movie mystique are fed with every new film released and continue to grow on their own as fans wait out the years until another fresh poster campaign, theme song, and Bond actress arise.

Smith 5

Works Cited

Collier, Aldore D. "Halle Berry Is the Sexy Bond Girl in Die Another Day." Jet 25 Nov. 2002: 58-63.

D'Abo, Maryam and John Cork. Bond Girls Are Forever: The Women of James Bond. New York: Harry N. Abrams, 2003.

Douglas, Susan J. Where the Girls Are: Growing Up Female with the Mass Media. New York: Times Books, 1994.

Nourmand, Tony. James Bond Movie Posters: The Official 007 Collection. San Francisco: Chronicle Books, 2002.

"Shirley Bassey." BBC. 2007. British Broadcasting Corporation. 19 Apr. 2007 <http://www.bbc.co.uk/wales/music/sites/ shirleybassey/pages/biography.shtml>.

Glossary of Usage

This glossary is a brief list of words and constructions that are commonly misused. Many of the texts in the Writing Center have somewhat longer lists. For a comprehensive list (dictionary), see Wilson Follett's Modern American Usage, a current edition of Webster's Collegiate Dictionary, or The American Heritage Dictionary of the English Language.

A, An: Before words that begin with a vowel sound (a-e-i-o-u), the proper form is "an." EXAMPLE: An eagle is a bird that lives in an aerie.

Abbreviations: Use abbreviations sparingly because they may confuse readers.

Accept, Except: "Accept" is a verb that means *to receive willingly*; "except" as a verb means *to exclude* and as a preposition means *but*. EX: I accept your explanation, but school officials will except each student who cheated on the test. All teachers except Ms. Johnston agreed with this policy.

Adapt, Adept, Adopt: "Adapt" means *to adjust or change*; "adept" means *skillful*; "adopt" means *to accept or make one's own*. EX: The intern adapted his own procedures so adeptly that the entire company may adopt his methods.

Adverse, Averse: "Adverse" means *unfavorable*. "Averse" means *opposed or reluctant* and is often followed by *to*. EX: Because that ingredient might cause an adverse reaction, we are averse to its use in the product.

Advice, Advise: "Advice" is a noun; "advise" is a verb. EX: Our advice is that officers advise suspects of their rights.

Affect, Effect: "Affect" is usually a verb; "effect" is usually a noun. EX: The rain affects me, but it has no significant effect on my dog.

Aid, Aide: "Aid" means *to help or to assist* as a verb and *a device or method of assistance* as a noun; an "aide" is a person. EX: The staff aids new aides by showing them visual aids as part of orientation.

Aisle, Isle: "Aisle" means *a passageway or row* as in "The store's aisles have been widened." "Isle" means *a small island* as in "We will meet at the isle closest to the beach."

All ready, Already: "All ready" indicates *everything or everyone is prepared*; "already" is a reference to time meaning *previously*. EX: Tom had already packed long before his teammates were all ready to leave.

All right, NOT Alright: Use "all right" instead of the nonstandard "alright." EX: The captain declared herself all right and fit for the volleyball tournament.

Allusion, Illusion: An "allusion" is *an indirect reference*; an "illusion" is *a false or misleading idea or image*. EX: The governor made an allusion to the concept of manifest destiny in his speech about the economy. The chorus of boos that followed showed that some people in the crowd feel his notion is an illusion unsuited for this state.

A lot, NOT Alot: EX: Monique spent a lot of time preparing for her interview.

Altar, Alter: "Altar" is a noun meaning *an elevated place or structure used in religious ceremonies*; "alter" is a verb meaning *to change*. EX: Because architects altered the plans, the altar was moved to the front right of the church's sanctuary.

Among, Between: Use "among" for three or more things or persons and "between" for two items. EX: Judges noted several winning dishes among the record number of submissions. As for my favorite, I found it difficult to choose between the lasagna and the pizza.

Amount, Number: "Amount" refers to *the quantity or mass of something*; "number" is used for countable things. EX: A large number of protesters turned out for such a small amount of exposure.

Angel, Angle: Don't make spelling mistakes that confuse *a spiritual being or heavenly messenger* with *a mathematical figure or*

measurement. To write, "My little sister was the cutest angle in the pageant" or "I carefully calibrated the designs down to the last angel" invites ridicule.

Anxious, Eager: These words are not interchangeable. "Anxious" means *distressed or worried;* "eager" means *having an intense interest or impatient desire.* EX: Although Floyd was anxious all morning, Lucinda was eager to begin the spelling bee.

Any one, Anyone: Use "any one" when making a specific reference to an individual entity; use "anyone" when the reference is not to any specific individual. EX: Anyone may audition for any one of the roles.
NOTE: The same guideline applies to "any body – anybody," "every body – everybody," and "every one – everyone."

Anywhere, NOT Anywheres: The preferred, standard form of this word should NOT contain the –s at the end. EX: Anywhere I turned, the children were watching my every move.
NOTE: Likewise, use "anyway," "backward," "forward," "nowhere," "toward," "way," and so on with no –s at the end of each word.

As: Do not use "as" for a causal reference in sentences like, "As it was raining, the game was postponed." Use "because" or "since" in those instances.
NOTE: The same guideline applies to the phrase "being that." Avoid using this phrase in your writing.

Assure, Ensure, Insure: These words all mean *to make certain or secure.* However, only "assure" is used in the sense of *putting the mind at rest,* and only "insure" is used in the sense of *guaranteeing property or persons against risk.* EX: To ensure against loss if our teenager has a fender-bender, the agent assured me that we need to be adequately insured.

Back up, Backup: "Back up" is a verb phrase; "backup" is a noun meaning *a duplicate or substitute, a supporting entity,* or *an overflow or accumulation.* EX: It's a good thing Veronica made a backup of the proposal. When a city worker backed up a truck near the interstate, he hit a telephone pole, knocking the pole across the freeway. Now Steve, along with the original copy, is stuck in the backup.

Bad, Badly: Use "bad" as an adjective and "badly" as an adverb. EX: Willis felt bad *(adjective that modifies the noun Willis)* about missing the party, but Moua told him the band was loud and played badly *(adverb that modifies the verb played)* all night.

Beside, Besides: "Beside" means *by the side of or next to*; "besides" means *in addition to or except.* EX: Besides the pitcher of water, Aunt Sally also placed a clean glass on the table beside the bed.

Borrow, Lend/Loan: "Borrow" means *to obtain or receive something or to adopt something as one's own*; "lend" or "loan" means *to give or provide something.* EX: If you lend me your textbook today, you can borrow my notes from the class you missed last week.

Capital, Capitol: "Capitol" refers to a building; "Capital" is used for all other meanings (money or resources, a city, etc.). EX: The capitol is in dire need of capital improvements.

Cite, Sight, Site: As with other homonyms (see later entry), these words have very different meanings. "Cite" means *to refer to or quote an authority*; "sight" means *seeing or a view that is seen*; "site" means *a particular location or place.* EX: At the site of the ancient ruins, the guide cited several experts to explain the origins of that stunning sight.

Climactic, Climatic: "Climactic" is derived from "climax" and refers to *a point of great intensity or culmination*; "climatic" pertains to climate. EX: The company's climactic decision to "go green" was in direct response to concerns about climatic changes.

Complement, Compliment: "Complement" deals with *completing or going along with something*; "compliment" deals with *expressing praise or flattery.* EX: The guests complimented their hosts on the rich cheesecake, the perfect complement to the delicious dinner.

Conscience, Conscious: The noun "conscience" refers to *the awareness of morality and ethics*, often thought of as the ability to know right from wrong; the adjective "conscious" refers to *being alert or aware physically and/or mentally.* EX: The experienced detective was conscious of the suspect's nervous behavior, perhaps revealing a guilty conscience.

Contractions: Formed by combining and shortening two words through the use of an apostrophe that replaces omitted letters (for instance, can + not becomes can't), "contractions" are a regular part of most speech. Writers of formal essays and documents are often advised to curtail the use of contractions because they can connote too casual a tone.

Could not care less, NOT Could care less: Use "not" in this expression because it correctly indicates the *apparent lack of concern or interest* intended by this phrase. EX: Jose insisted he could not care less about the new boss. "I plan to keep working hard," he said.

Council, Counsel: A "council" is *a group of people (councilors) who serve in some legislative or administrative body*; "counsel" means *advice or to advise,* and those who offer such guidance may be called *counselors* (hence the term *counselor* is sometimes used for a lawyer). EX: The city council retains a lawyer to provide legal counsel.

Deadwood (Wordiness): Noun phrases that include terms like "manner," "nature," and "type" are frequently meaningless and awkward. Instead of writing, "She dances in a beautiful manner," or "It is the very nature of football to be a violent sport," write, "She dances beautifully," and "Football is a violent sport."

Decent, Descent: "Decent" is an adjective meaning *proper, acceptable, morally upright, or kind*; "descent" is a noun meaning *the act or process of going downward or declining.* EX: Our neighbor was a decent fellow until his descent into drug abuse.

Defiantly, Definitely: These adverbs have very different meanings, "defiantly" referring to *a bold resistance or opposition* and "definitely" referring to *precision, distinctness, or certainty.* EX: The Masked Avenger defiantly shook his fist at the pro wrestling fans, shouting, "You have definitely not seen the last of me!"

Desert, Dessert: The extra –s is a good memory device—many people want an extra serving of a good "dessert." "Desert" as a noun usually means *a barren, dry area* and as a verb means *to abandon or leave*. EX: The one thing that kept me from deserting our family Sunday dinners was my mother's spectacular desserts.

Device, Devise: "Device" is a noun; "devise" is a verb.
EX: I'd like to talk to the person who devised the cell phone, one of the most annoying devices ever created.

Dual, Duel: "Dual" means *composed of two or having a double purpose*; "duel" means *a formal combat or a struggle, or engaging in such*. EX: The weekend snowball duels served dual aims—getting the kids outside for exercise and giving the weary parents a little peace.

Each and Every: In the sentence, "I love you more each and every day," this phrase is redundant. Use one or the other of these words, not both. EX: I love you more every day.

Each, Every, Everyone: These are singular pronouns and accompany singular verbs and pronouns. Thus, "Each of the girls drives her own car," NOT "Each of the girls drive their own cars."

Elicit, Illicit: The verb "elicit" means *to bring forth or evoke*; the adjective "illicit" means *unlawful or not permitted*. EX: At the organic garden club's monthly meeting, the president announced the resignation of a long-time member because of her illicit use of chemical fertilizer. This shocking disclosure elicited gasps of disbelief from the other gardeners.

Emigrate, Immigrate: The first term means *to leave one's homeland and settle in another country*; the second term means *to enter and reside in another country*. EX: The Xiongs, who live across the street, emigrated from Laos three decades ago and have become citizens of the United States. They should not be carelessly lumped together with people who have immigrated here illegally.

Eminent, Imminent: Though both words are adjectives, "eminent" means *prominent, noteworthy, outstanding or distinguished*, and imminent means *impending or about to occur*. EX: Harold Russell, the eminent novelist and human rights advocate, will speak at the library. His imminent arrival has the staff scurrying in preparation.

Father, Mother: These words are often preferred, especially in instances when you want to convey a more formal and/or respectful (not necessarily stuffy) tone. "Dad" and "Mom" convey a tone that is more casual and familiar.
NOTE: Capitalize these words only when used as names. EX: My dad says that Mother has the kindest smile he has ever seen.

Fewer, Less: "Fewer" modifies countable nouns; "less" modifies mass (non-countable) nouns. EX: Francine practiced fewer hours than Charlie, but Charlie has less experience in pressure situations.

Firstly, Secondly, Thirdly: The –ly ending in these words is pretentious. Instead, use "first," "second," "third," and so on.

Formally, Formerly: "Formally" refers to *something formal or established by custom or rule*; "formerly" means *previously.*
EX: Dr. Otumba, formerly of Hope Hospital, even dresses formally on weekends.

Good, Well: Used as descriptive terms, "good" is an adjective and "well" an adverb. EX: Mai felt good about her first recital. She performed well even though she was the initial pianist on the program.

Height, Width: There is no –h at the end of "height."
EX: The carpenter measured the height of the barn but neglected to note the barn's width.

Himself, NOT Hisself: EX: Mario found himself lost after making several wrong turns.

Homonyms: "Homonyms" are words that sound like other words but are spelled differently and have different meanings. You will <u>not</u> detect homonym errors simply by employing a spell-check tool while word processing. Use a dictionary and thesaurus in combination to discover usage errors. Some of the entries in this glossary are homonyms, but there are many, many more that are not listed and discussed. Following are just some of the troublesome homonyms that may lead to errors: *are-hour-our; bare-bear; brake-break; do-due; faint-feint; grate-great; hear-here; loan-*

lone; meat-meet; pain-pane; pedal-peddle-petal; poor-pore-pour; rain-reign-rein; sew-so-sow; stationary-stationery; and *vain-vein.*

Hopefully: This adverb means something is done *in a hopeful manner.* EX: Despite having no guarantees about the completion date from the contractor, they hopefully entered the renovated cabin.
NOTE: To avoid confusion about who is doing the hoping, do <u>not</u> write sentences such as, "Hopefully, the package will arrive on time." Instead, write, "I hope the package will arrive on time."

In conclusion: Do not use this unnecessary phrase.

In my opinion, I would like to say: Omit these unnecessary references to yourself. These are implied because you are writing the paper.

It's, Its: "It's" = It is. "Its" signals possession. EX: It's a skunk, not a cat. Look at the streak on its back.

Kind of, Sort of: These expressions should be used to indicate *type or category.* EX: *What sort of car do you want to buy?*
NOTE: Avoid using "kind of" or "sort of" as casual expressions to mean *fairly, rather, somewhat* in sentences such as "The Smiths were kind of surprised to see us at the airport." Instead, write, "The Smiths were rather surprised to see us at the airport."

Lead, Led: As a noun, "lead" is a mineral, for instance, the lead that might be used in a heavy weight or doorstop. EX: My grandfather used to employ large lead sinkers when fishing in the deep part of the lake. As a verb in the present tense, "to lead" means *to provide direction.* EX: Wherever the guide leads the visitors, they will follow him. In the past tense, however, the standard form is "led." EX: The Pied Piper led his followers into the river.

Lie, Lay: As a verb, "lie" can mean *to recline;* "lay" means *to place or put down.* The past tense of "lie" is "lay," and "laid" is the past tense of "lay." EX: I often lie on the couch when I'm tired. This morning I lay down for an hour. Afterwards, I laid some tile in the basement.

Like: Although "like" as a conjunction is gaining currency in speech, it is not acceptable in formal usage. The standard variety, then, is "The meal tasted good, as (not *like*) home cooked meals often do." Substitute "as," "as if," "as though," or "in the way" whenever one of these forms will work in place of "like."

Literally: "Literally" means *word-for-word, actually or really, strictly.* EX: Some justices have been criticized for too literally interpreting the language of the Constitution's authors.
NOTE: One of the most abused of adverbs, "literally" too often has been inaccurately employed by writers to express an idea that is meant "figuratively" as in a figure of speech. Instead of writing, "Uncle Ned was laughing so hard, he was literally beside himself," which is not literally possible (another Uncle Ned suddenly appeared?), just eliminate the offending word. EX: Uncle Ned was laughing so hard, he was beside himself. OR Uncle Ned was beside himself with laughter.

Looking to, Fixing to: Avoid such overly casual phrases in sentences such as, "I was looking to get a summer job before I was fixing to visit my cousins in Tennessee." EX: I wanted to get a summer job before visiting my cousins in Tennessee.

Loose, Lose: "Loose" is an adjective; "lose" is a verb.
EX: Tamika tightened the loose rope so that she would not lose the mattress on the drive to her sister's apartment across town.

May be, Maybe: The verb phrase "may be" is not the same as the adverb "maybe," which means *possibly.* EX: "We may be able to reserve the ballroom after all," Albert said. "Maybe we should call the manager and explain the mix-up."

Media, Medium: Don't confuse these nouns. "Medium" is singular, and "media" is plural. EX: As the award-winning painter Ricardo Mantares explained to the assembled members of the media, his favorite medium in art school was watercolor.

Moral, Morale: "Moral" as a noun means *a lesson or a standard of conduct* and as an adjective means *concerned with goodness or badness in character or behavior.* "Morale" is a noun meaning *spirit, mood or attitude.* EX: If the managers did not conduct themselves in a moral manner, the morale in this office would crumble.

Most: "Most" is nonstandard and should be avoided in sentences such as "Most everyone I know will be there." Instead, write, "Almost everyone I know will be there."

Names and Acronyms: In formal writing, names of individuals who are not of close acquaintance are usually written out completely on first reference (*President Abraham Lincoln*) and are referred to by last name (*Lincoln*) subsequently. The same is true for businesses, agencies, organizations, and so on. An "acronym," *a word formed from the first letters of names with multiple words*, is generally acceptable after the first reference. EX: The National Football League is the most financially successful sports organization in the world. It is practically impossible to lose money as the owner of an NFL franchise.

Of: "Would of," "could of," and "should of" are misspellings. The correct second word in each phrase is "have." The proper spelling of these contractions is "would've," "could've," and "should've."

Passed, Past: "Passed" is always used as a verb; "past" can be a noun (*the distant past*), an adjective (*past president*), an adverb (*strolled past*), or preposition (*past noon*) but not a verb. EX: Otis learned from his past mistakes. This semester, he studied hard and easily passed all of his classes.

Percent, Percentage: "Percent" is always used *in reference to a specific number;* when *no number is specified,* "percentage" is used. EX: The rate of crime downtown rose 125 percent since 2005. Of the crimes tallied, only a small percentage involved guns.
NOTE: In formal writing, use the word instead of the % symbol.

Perfect, Unique: Being "more perfect" or "most unique" is impossible. "Perfect" is *the best something can be,* and "unique" indicates something is *one of a kind.* You cannot have more than the best possible or the most in terms of uniqueness. Additionally, many writers overuse these terms. Be sure to understand the formal definitions of words such as "unique" and "perfect" before using them in your writing.

Persecute, Prosecute: "Persecute" means *to harass persistently;* "prosecute" means *to carry out legal action against someone.*

EX: The bully persecuted the owners of the deli for years. The entire neighborhood was pleased when he was prosecuted and convicted for vandalizing their storefront.

Precede, Proceed: "Precede" means *to come before or in front of*; "proceed" means *to move on, go forward, or continue*.
EX: The legislators must discuss what preceded the budget negotiations if the hearing is to proceed as scheduled.

Principal, Principle: "Principal" means *highest in rank, importance or worth* as an adjective; as a noun, "principal" can refer to *the head of a school, a main or leading participant, or the amount of debt not counting the interest*. "Principle" is a noun meaning *a basic truth, a standard or rule, an essential quality*. EX: "The principal reason we are here," said the new middle school principal, "is to establish sound principles of learning and citizenship."

Quiet, Quite: Beware typos with these words! "Quiet" refers to *the absence of noise, calmness or serenity, being free of trouble*; "quite" is an adverb meaning *completely, to an extreme or a certain degree, actually or really*. EX: The witness said she was quite certain the bartender was quiet and did nothing to provoke the fight with the unruly patron.

Real, Really: "Real" is an adjective; "really" is an adverb.
EX: Just hearing the slogan for Mom's Café, "Real food at really yummy prices," invariably makes me really hungry.

Really: In sentences such as "I really find science labs to be boring," or "The concert was really exciting," "really" is not a particularly meaningful term. Think consciously about the necessity of this word before using it in formal writing.

Reason is because, Reason why: The verb "is" followed by an adverb ("because," "when," "where," etc.) usually results in an awkward sentence. The word "because" implies an explanation, so "reason" and "why" make for exceedingly redundant phrasing. Instead of writing, "The reason why Joe drank is because he had nothing else to do," write, "Joe drank because he had nothing else to do."

Redundancies: Phrases like "true fact," "past history," "future prospects," or "personal opinion" are unnecessary. For example, "history" means "past," making the combination of the two redundant. A basic principle of style is to cut a word whenever you can do so without loss of meaning.

Regardless, NOT Irregardless: "Regardless" means *in spite of everything.* EX: The farmers must get into the fields regardless of the weather forecast.

Set, Sit: Use "set" when you mean *to place* and "sit" when you mean *to be seated.* EX: After the table is set for Thanksgiving dinner, Grandma Betty always sits at the dining room chair nearest to the kitchen.

So: Do not overuse "so" as a conjunction: "Ted pulled a muscle, so he didn't suit up for the game." Either choose a more precise connective, or rewrite the sentence in a different way: "Having pulled a muscle, Ted didn't even suit up for the game." Some writers also mistakenly use "so" as a substitute for "very," as in "The waves cresting white were so beautiful." Finally, the term that introduces a result is "so that," not "so," as in "He arranged the chairs so that every student could see every other student."

Some time, Sometime: "Some time" means *a period or duration of time*; "sometime" refers to *an unspecified point in time.* EX: Graciela has not seen her cousins for some time, but she plans on visiting them sometime next month.

Suppose(d), Use(d): The proper spelling is "supposed" and "used" in sentences such as "He is supposed to be here," and "They are used to these conditions."
NOTE: Writers sometimes mistake the proper ending as –ably for the adverb form of such words. Use –edly to be correct. EX: The treasure was supposedly placed somewhere in this park. The winning medallion will undoubtedly be found here tomorrow.

Sure to/Try to, NOT Sure and/Try and: These sentences are incorrect: "I will be sure and write my congressperson. She must try and understand how her constituents feel about this issue." Instead, write "sure to" and "try to."

Than, Then: "Than" is used in comparisons; "then" means *at that time*. EX: The demolition crew was no more than two blocks away. The foreman hit the switch, and then the bridge collapsed.

Their, There, They're: "Their" is *a plural possessive pronoun.* "There" is *a place*, as in "He lives there." This form is also *a grammatical device used to introduce sentences*, as in "There was a tavern in a town." Finally, "they're" is *the contraction of they are.* EX: There is only one way to cross to their property on the hill over there.

Themselves, NOT Theirselves: EX: They had no one to blame but themselves for missing the deadline.

'Til, Until: Use "until" unless you are quoting dialogue. "'Til" is nonstandard. EX: Tony waited until the speakers went on sale before purchasing them.

To, Too, Two: "To" is used as part of an infinitive phrase (to strive, to seek, to find, and not to yield) or as a preposition (to the bank, to Center City). "Too" means *excessively* (too late, too expensive) or *also* (He came, too). "Two" = 2. EX: We returned the book to the reserve desk two minutes before closing time. "You're cutting it a little too close," said the head librarian.

Weather, Whether: "Weather" is a noun referring to *the state of the atmosphere*; "whether" is a conjunction used to *introduce an alternative or choices*. EX: Whether held in the gym or at the stadium, the festival will go on no matter what kind of weather the day brings.
NOTE: "Or not" is often not necessary with "whether" to show the alternative choice. In "We questioned whether or not we should bring an extra chair," "or not" can be cut to be less wordy.

Well: The interjection "well" ("Well, I declare"), though appropriate in speech, is generally inappropriate in formal writing.

While: This word means *at the same time*. EX: While Tyler painted the front porch, Marissa planted flowers.
NOTE: Do <u>not</u> use it to mean *although, whereas,* or *on the other hand* because it can be confusing. In "Faulkner wrote long convoluted sentences while Twain wrote simple, concise

sentences," "while" might mistakenly be thought to mean *simultaneously* by some readers (these authors wrote in different time periods).

Who's, Whose: "Who's" is *the contraction for who is*; "whose" is *a possessive pronoun*. EX: Who's going to decide whose concept will be chosen for the new ad campaign?

You know: This phrase is inappropriate in academic writing.

You're, Your: "You're" is *the contraction for you are*; "your" is *a possessive pronoun*: EX: "I like your drive, your attitude, your experience," said the owner. "You're an excellent candidate to join this firm."